Girl from Fitchburg

GIRL *from* FITCHBURG

Bernardine Kielty Scherman

Random House New York

TO

Harry

CONTENTS

❀ *Part One* ❀

WAY BACK

I

A TOWN TO GROW
UP IN

If you let yourself sink farther and farther back into the past, a world almost forgotten comes gradually to the surface. Names and places emerge, faraway sounds and sights bob up like corks. People you would have thought lost forever come back to life. It is slow magic.

This happened to me as I thought about Fitchburg . . .

Fitchburg was a mill town, typical industrial New England fifty miles from Boston. The Nashua River was a miniature Merrimack, as Fitchburg itself was a smaller Lowell, Lawrence or Haverhill—but of the same family. Machinery clanked day in day out, and the *clop-clop* of workmen's feet echoed through the dark streets before sunrise and after sunset. Alvah Crocker started the first paper mill in 1826, and in so doing established the solid wealth of the town and its most powerful dynasty. (Both Crockers and paper mills are still going strong.) Later came the gingham mills, woolen mills, machine shops, foundries. By 1883 Fitchburg had supplied machinery for some of the largest paper mills, not only in the United States but in Canada and Japan as well. The Putnam Machine Company furnished the first two fully equipped machine shops in China. The Dickensons made shoes, the Lowes owned the textile mills, Simonds was famous for saws. These were not Brahmin names in the Boston sense, but they were good mercantile New England, to which were added the French Canadian Perault, iron foundry; the Irish Dillon, steel boilers; the Swedish Iver Johnson, bicycles and revolvers.

The men, women and children who ran the machines that made the mills go round were the Irish who had been coming over in masses from 1835 on, the Germans who came around 1848, and the French who dribbled down from Canada. The Germans made up the bulk of skilled mechanics, and the Canucks, as they were called, the ordinary mill workers.

A district grew up at the south end of town known as the Patch, to which the Irish gravitated, making up the big parish of St. Bernard's; and in West Fitchburg, crowded around the Andrew Cleghorn mill, was "Cleghorn" which harbored the French Canadians. Cleghorn had its own church and school and language, and was a place apart.

Swedes lived near the mills in ungainly three-story wooden tenements, their piazzas and outside stairways unpainted and rickety but scrupulously clean, with a hospitable whiff of coffee in the air. The Germans made sausage and played the trombone and cornet. Indeed, in the days of my childhood a Kimball Street sausage-maker played first trombone in the Boston Symphony Orchestra—though I only learned of this later.

. . .

At the turn of the century Fitchburg was a proper town to be brought up in, the right size to attract all kinds. It had a population of around thirty thousand, and there was a variety of small commercial enterprises to fill the needs of that many people—businesses that on the whole required no special ingenuity. Competition was not wearing, and fathers provided their families with an entirely adequate income for a contentedly busy life.

Mothers usually did their own cooking and sewing, with considerable pride in achievement: dressmaking at home and what we now call regional cooking. Except for the cheapest of work dresses and the costliest gowns, ready-made dresses were a rarity. There was no quick turnover of seasonal styles in those days, and a girl's dress was likely to express her mother's individuality, with the loving extras of hemstitching and smocking and shirring that none but the finest couturier would bother with today. Underwear was handmade, with ribbons that ran all through the embroidery of chemises and corset covers and nightgowns, and had to be taken out and reinserted after each laundering.

Time was not a factor. Beans soaked all night Friday and baked all day Saturday. Hot muffins were commonplace for breakfast. Cottage pudding, hot and light, was a favorite noontime dessert, served with foamy sauce. Or baked Indian pudding as yellow as maize. Or dark rich mince pie. Sunday suppers, which modern households try to skip, were savory with scalloped oysters or crusty browned hash. Nothing was too much trouble. Nor do I recall a single person complaining of indigestion. "Dyspepsia" was a word for the comics.

In these middle-class families that made up the bulk of the town, boys took jobs in summer cutting grass, and delivered papers all year round. Tossing the *Sentinel* from a moving bike to a side porch was an art that took practice.

Throughout that part of Massachusetts the public schools were first-rate, and in Fitchburg everybody attended them. The Crocker family, by now the town's old aristocrats, with several collateral houses grouped on top of the Prospect Street hill, did not send their children to public schools. They had governesses at home and later went away to boarding school. St. Bernard's Irish Catholic parish maintained a parochial school, as did the French in Cleghorn. But their pupils were few in number. The French Canadians ducked school altogether, when they could, in favor of working in the mills, child-labor laws notwithstanding, and the majority of Irish children went to public schools, as did the rest of the town's children without further exception. It was good to grow up with all kinds and all nationalities.

My "best" friends around the age of ten represented that whole little world. Kalla Peterson was a Swedish child whose older sister Marta was already working in one of the gingham mills. Though I was in and out of Kalla's house often—a third-floor tenement near the mill—I rarely saw her sister or her brothers or her father. They all went to work before six-thirty in the morning and worked until six at night.

Equally close was Constance Savage, who lived in a big house on Prospect Street and whose family had three or four neat Irish maids and a huge Saint Bernard named Duke. Duke was well known throughout our part of town for his daily raids on garbage pails, and his house in Connie's backyard was our special hiding place. There we would sit, two or three of us, tight and close, amidst the fleas, telling secrets.

Alice Conn's father owned a grocery store, and early in the afternoon on drowsy summer days Mr. Conn would let us two little girls play real store—weigh out rice and dried peas and coffee beans for a line of imaginary customers.

Dorothy Shea, whose father owned a quarry on solid-granite Rollstone Hill, was perhaps a year older than I but a close companion. Her father, I think, must have been an "Irish patriot," for she used to quote him about the poor Irish. "Just one grain of corn, Mother, just one grain of corn!" she would recite melodramatically, but neither of us saw any connection between ourselves and the pale wraith that we conjured up—especially since Dorothy herself was affluent. She had ten cents to spend where none of the others among us ever had more than five. Where we would buy penny candies for bulk, she would discriminate and on Saturdays invest in a quarter pound of candy known as "opera chocolates," which I believe even now to have been above average.

"Nested among her hills she lies, The city of our love!" We all learned it at school along with the story of John Fitch's abduction by Indians in 1756. —Like Rome, Fitchburg was built on seven hills, and level ground was scarce. The entire length of Main Street ran parallel to the river. The middle section was lined with the best stores, and the street ended uptown in the Common. The Common, usually the pretty center of a New England town, lost something in Fitchburg by not lying flat. It had a plain, rather undistinguished fountain designed by Herbert Adams, the local sculptor, a few gravel paths, sparse grass because of the shade trees, and benches with the green paint worn off. But on Tuesday nights in summer, when the Fitchburg Military Band played a concert, it was a place of enchantment. I can still hear "The Anvil Chorus" floating out from the

brightly lighted bandstand to the shadowed figures that
wandered blissfully under the elms and the maples . . .
"The Blue Bells of Scotland" . . . "The Angels' Serenade"
in a piercingly sweet cornet solo.

Halfway up Main Street was Monument Square, surrounded by important buildings: the Court House; Christ's
Church Episcopal, ivy-covered; the Wallace Library. In the
center of the square stood the Soldiers' Monument. I knew
that my grandfather Kielty's name was engraved on one of
the four bronze tablets that listed the hundred and thirty-
five Fitchburg men who had died in the Civil War, but I
don't recollect ever having read it, a childhood negligence
that I look back on with dismay. In 1962 I read it with
pride.

Somewhere along Main Street stood the old Whitney
Opera House where, before my time, the eminent of the
American stage had played their parts. James O'Neill in
The Count of Monte Cristo, Joseph Jefferson in *Rip Van
Winkle*, Richard Mansfield, Wilton Lackaye. These names
I could only have heard from my parents' lips, but they
breathed that indefinable glamor which for me the theater
has never lost. Out of the haze come names of plays like
Trilby and *Zaza*, suggestive of a strange and sinister world
far removed from Fitchburg.

Since those days I have learned that the Whitney
Opera House was a sound commercial enterprise known to
the booking trade in its heyday as a "good-paying house."
Its seating capacity was a thousand, and in 1886, for instance, it put on ninety-two evening performances and eight
matinées, grossing $25,000.

What I do remember out of my own experience is the
days when the old Opera House had degenerated into a
"Ten-Twenty-Thirt' "—orchestra seats thirty cents, balcony
twenty, and family circle ten. The family circle of a Saturday afternoon overflowed with children staring down at the

distant stage from hard wooden seats with iron armrests. A vivid recollection persists of a pale black-haired lady in yellow satin stretched over a saw, the blade of which was moving with painful, slow inevitability toward her white neck. I think it may have been *Nellie the Sewing-Machine Girl.* The horrors of present-day television can be no worse, nor will they be longer remembered.

Uncle Tom's Cabin, a perennial, was very sad. We always cried at Uncle Tom's quiet nobility, and when little Eva rose to heaven, as she miraculously did, we believed— though she never got quite as high as the top balcony.

City Hall was—and is—an austerely simple building in good early-nineteenth-century tradition. It had a large hall on the second floor that in those days extended its entire width, with long many-paned windows. I went to Children's Parties there, and once to a big Scottish get-together with bagpipes and kilts, probably organized by the remnant of Scotch weavers still left in the Fitchburg mills.

There were more horse-drawn carriages in those days than automobiles, and people still laughed as cars chugged up the steep hills. We had a buggy with small wheels and rubber tires, and a horse named Bessie. On summer evenings my father and I used to drive out Lunenburg way on good dirt roads, in that mysterious hour between sunset and dark. In winter we whizzed along in a low sleigh, a heavy rug over our legs, and fur cap and gloves on head and hands. The evergreen branches traced with snow, the tingling cold on the cheeks, the balls of ice kicked up by Bessie—who loved it as much as we did!—are things never to be forgotten. Nor the warm steamy smell of the barn on our return, when my father unharnessed Bessie in the lantern light and rubbed her down. She had a box stall because she was so precious.

Maybe my parents knew that I went to the "Ten-Twenty-Thirt'," and maybe they didn't. The figure of

Dorothy Shea with her bag of chocolates, certainly more worldly and a wee bit older, looms as the one who may have taken me. But on the whole we children of Fitchburg were free as the wind. We roamed the town playing fox and hounds, leaving a trail of chalk arrows to show our direction. When I see chalk arrows on a sidewalk now, I wonder if anyone still plays fox and hounds, and—appalling thought!—if they play it in the streets of New York. We did not really go all over Fitchburg, but we covered a wide territory with an abandon that must have been good for our souls. When my own children were growing up I tried, nostalgically, to give them that same freedom, but I'm afraid it figured out as carelessness in my guardianship.

We thought we were free as the wind. But actually we obeyed our parents and respected our teachers. A sound Yankee self-discipline was instilled in us at an early age. We did what we had to do but didn't want to do: that was life. And no matter how far from New England, it's my belief that we who were brought up that way still find it hard to shake off that philosophy. A Yankee seems to have been born to a distrust of casual unpremeditated enjoyment. He does not read for pleasure in the morning, candy before lunch is scandalous, and music, if any, is for evenings. And he finishes the book he is reading whether he likes it or not.

But what fun we had in our mild escape from authority—riding our bicycles like acrobats, down the hills with feet on the front-wheel stirrups, on level ground without either hands or feet touching; or hopping the rear step of Green's Ice Wagon as it rumbled over the cobbles, pulled by a team of white horses, the iceman brandishing his whip in vain to get us off.

Winters were long and cold and exhilarating. From December to March we went sliding. "Sliding" was on a sled, most girls sitting up primly, the boys going belly-bumps. "Coasting" was a term never used in Fitchburg, and "sleighing" was behind a horse.

Skating on the mill pond in the late winter afternoons, the streaks of rose on the sunset clouds, the darkening sky, and the light from hundreds of factory windows shimmering across the ice—that was a true esthetic experience which left an indelible impression on an ordinary little schoolgirl. Not long ago my husband and I were walking along Park Avenue in New York at that same hour. The glass buildings were ablaze with changing light and color. We both exclaimed at the beauty. But in the same instant I was skating again—cold, awkward, happy—in the patterned brightness of the Parkhill mill.

Fitchburg had a hotel, the American House, with wide steps on which characters lounged. This was where the "drummers" were said to stay, and although the American House existed all the years I lived in Fitchburg I never went inside it, nor do I know anyone who did. Drummers were unspeakables. I imagine that to have had that kind of job they were full of gusto, and probably brought a breath of city life to small merchants in dull towns where gusto was at a premium. It was a mild era. The everyday supply of young men of that pre-automobile age must have been pretty placid beside today's junior salesmen, garage mechanics, or construction gangs in helmets. A world upheaval separates these "tough guys" from the Fitchburg locals, just as it does City Markets and Food Fairs from the Atlantic and Pacific Tea Company, which occupied a modest store on Main Street. There was no suggestion whatsoever of future A & P efficiency in the way it ran its business. The "order man" came round to all the customers' houses and took orders for coffee (Mocha and Java) and tea. He was quite a talker and knew everybody's business—a vestige of the old-time peddler.

One of Fitchburg's landmarks was the depot. In railroad circles the Fitchburg Division of the Boston & Maine was quite a road. Again Alvah Crocker was responsible. Fitchburg must have its outlet to the sea, said he, got it put through the state legislature in spite of opposition and ridicule, and rode into town himself on the first locomotive (March 5, 1845).

On its trip west the train passed the old stone Fitchburg Depot right outside Boston's North Station where Jenny Lind once sang, ran through Waltham where watches were made, Concord with its battle, Walden Pond with Thoreau, then after Fitchburg by way of North Adams to Saratoga Springs—the shortest route from the "Hub" to the "Spa." Through Bellows Falls, Vermont, it ran to fashionable Lake George. The smell of smoke and cinders, and the steam that enveloped someone standing on the bridge under which the train ran, are a part of childhood. At night a train roared through town which they said went to Montreal—but I always doubted it.

The big brick depot seemed eternal, but alas! in 1962 it lay in a heap of rubble. It was built in 1877 with high ceilings, columns and arches, and a white-faced clock on the tall tower by which the town ran its business. In my day as many as fifty passenger trains arrived and departed daily. Now not fifty a week come in, and the smart morning train to Boston at 8 A.M. consists of a single car. Instead of a dignified building the proud railroad, still managing to keep alive but barely so, has one room in a restaurant beside the tracks for its waiting room and ticket office. The rear of a "diner" is all that is left for the historic old Fitchburg Division.

.   .   .

There was scarcely a trace of early American in Fitchburg. The wooden tenement houses of the poor covered it like a blanket. They lined the back streets, sometimes in double rows, the rear tenements a shade more ramshackle than those in front. I know about these, because, although born in Ireland, my great-aunt Catherine (Kielty) McCarty quickly took to the ways of the New World, and by the time I knew her, owned stretches of the unsanitary dismal Patch that brought her what in those days was quite a fortune. With a black bonnet tied around her hard unsmiling face she went about collecting her rents, well braced against any complaints from her miserable tenants, and, ironical for one of her background, ready to evict any who hadn't the cash ready.

The dignified houses of the well-to-do stood, decently spaced, along the streets parallel to Main Street in the north and up the hills on that side of town, culminating in the social pinnacle of Prospect Street. Though even the best of them would hardly qualify as "stately homes," they were large and comfortable and well built, usually with mansard roofs, often with porte-cocheres. Their lawns, although not broad, were always velvety, and their windows shining. The next level down, architecturally speaking, were more pretentious, combining shiny red brick and rough granite, with rounded piazzas, turrets, and broken surfaces of shingles. I remember only one house with columns of the Greek revival, and a lovely cool one it was under its elm trees. But scattered through the city were perhaps a half-dozen really old houses left over from a day of simpler and better taste —plain, well-proportioned structures with square, low-ceilinged rooms and small-paned windows. Somehow they had survived, as had, here and there, the strain of the high-minded Puritan. Antiques had not yet become a fad, and in general old furniture was thrown out for new. But in one or

two of these older houses the earlier mahogany had not
been replaced by carved ebony or fumed oak. These re-
minders of another day were scarcely noticed, and their
owners made no perceptible impression on the life of the
town. They comprised a small residue of intellectuals who
lived what I now imagine must have been a completely fulfilling existence quite apart from the main stream of the
bustling mill town. In those days I never gave them a
thought. It is only in looking back that I realize their niche.
For whom else did the Kneisel Quartet come regularly to
play their beautiful music in Wallace Hall? Who but one of
their number was responsible for the magnificent organ in
the Congregational Church and the good selections played
on it? Among them was a painter whose name meant little,
to me at least, until I learned many years later that she had
exhibited at the Paris Salon in 1886, and a hunchback poet
on Pritchard Street whose family seemed otherwise normal
. . . It was that kind of town—with all kinds of people.
And something of all that life rubbed off on the unwitting
young.

What we were most conscious of, however, was not
the past but the present, not culture but immediate pleasure.
And the scene of some of our greatest delights was Whalom.
Far and away the best trolley ride out of town was to
Whalom. The trolley got you there in fifteen minutes, and
if you were lucky you got a seat out front next to the motor-
man, the wind tearing through your hair. Only men and
boys sat in the corresponding seat in the rear, which was
the conductor's stand when he was not hanging perilously
on the narrow outside step collecting fares.

Whalom was a small pleasure park on a lake where
the young of Fitchburg bathed in the summer and skated
in the winter, where romantic lads and their girls went ca-

noeing summer evenings with the music of the merry-go-round coming out to them across the water. "Wait Till the Sun Shines, Nellie" . . . "Bill Bailey, Won't You Please Come Home? . . ."

Whalom is still there, but a hurricane blew down all the tall pine trees and a roller coaster clatters where the picnic tables once stood. It still has a theater, even listed in the New York Sunday paper's Straw-hat Circuit. But in the old days it was a cynosure for all summer theaters. Its stage was framed with rough-hewn logs, bark still on; the roof was high, and the sides were open to the fragrance of pines and the light of the moon.

Someone with rare good taste must have managed that rustic theater. There, at the turn of the century, one saw the best of Gilbert & Sullivan (with, I think, Rose Coghlan as Buttercup), *The Bohemian Girl* ("I Dreamt that I Dwelt in Ma-arble Halls . . ."), *The Grand Duchess* ("The sabre, the sabre . . ."), *Giroflé-Girofla* (the twins), *Beautiful Galatea* (the statue that came to life!), *Fra Diavolo, The Mascot.*

They were effervescent light operas that swept the continent of Europe in the seventies and eighties, written by such masters of the craft as Offenbach, Auber, LeCoq, von Suppé. Few present could have had a notion of it then, certainly not I, but a shiver still runs up my spine at the mention of these delectable musical bonbons. They were the Great World, quite understandably never to be within reach, but gazed upon so appreciatively from afar.

One marvels at the rightness of Whalom Park for the young. It was so stimulating, so gay, so innocent.

Not everything was so innocent in those days. In a town that size, people's sins are pretty well known. Most indiscretions get thoroughly aired. Yet I am scandalized in my maturity to think of the items that I picked up as a

small child—that perhaps all children pick up, especially
girls. It raises the question, as it did with my own children,
of talking freely before the young. Is it better to let them
hear all, uncensored? Or should gossip and the prying into
motives and personalities that is so fascinating to grownups
be silenced when they appear? One hates to see those clear
brows contracted, and those innocent ideals tarnished. Yet
I am not sorry that I knew what I knew.

I knew for instance that the daughter of one of the
prominent families, respectably housed under her mansard
roof, was an alcoholic—a term that did not enter my vocabulary until about ten years ago. In those days they said "she
drank." They said it was temptation. Her parents were
wine drinkers and always left an open bottle on the side-
board. But *how did everybody know?*—The town boasted
two handsome young ministers, one ethereal, the other
dashing. Ladies buzzed about the worldly one, but whether
any real scandal touched him, or people were just on the
lookout, I don't know. Whatever his actions he was always
news. With the other, things were more serious. His fine
mind, his spirituality, must have unnerved the gossips. His
aloofness handicapped them. But he was an unhappy man,
I am sure, and looking back I feel that tragedy darkened
his quiet, dignified home.

More definite facts surround a certain lovely-looking
lady, an Edith Wharton heroine, slender, chestnut-haired
and exquisite, who never married but in her quiet deadli-
ness broke up the homes of two married couples. She
haunts me still with her pale-faced charm. There was the
story of the hardware-store owner and the mill girl, and of
the photographer and the singer—which gave picture-
taking a special thrill. A conspicuously wealthy married
citizen was involved with a pretty blonde for years. None
of these people did I know—really. No one actually ever

told me about their irregularities. I divined the nature of their sins, I imagine, from tones of voice. One man, from an exemplary family, was not only socially ostracized, he was banished from town. From the hush of horror in the voices, I knew why. I *almost* knew why. I'm sure it was twenty, maybe thirty, years before I ever heard the word "homosexual." Or "abortion." Yet I knew . . . But I never dwelt on these melodramas, nor felt the slightest emotion about any of those involved, except possibly the photographer. The only effect, I judge, was a certain inner satisfaction at "placing" things. Nothing more. Yet I do remember the misdeeds more vividly than the acts of charity.

Only last year in New York I met a man who asked me, when he learned the name of my home town, if I'd ever heard of a certain banker, whose name he mentioned. Surprisingly enough, I did remember that name, and before he told me, I knew that somehow that banker had been in serious trouble of the kind a banker can't afford. The very name brought back the face, the bank where he worked, the aura of sin. "Well, he was innocent!" my new acquaintance told me.

Financial shenanigans were rare in Fitchburg as topics of conversation. Affairs of the heart were not. And drunkenness, which in a factory city was an all-too-common tragedy, was a matter of frequent discussion. In those days Massachusetts had local option. Each city voted on prohibition, and when prohibition won out at election time, all the church bells rang for joy—a joy that was echoed in the hearts of the workingmen's families and spread throughout the whole rather smug middle stratum. For a year at least no liquor could be sold. The mill hands and the foundry workers would come home each week with their pay envelopes intact.

The outside world hardly penetrated. But I do remember children shouting in games, "Run or the Spaniards will get you!" One notable evening a brightly lighted battleship ran through town on the trolley tracks followed by a rousing torchlight procession, to which nothing in our modern celebrations is comparable. That must have been a tribute to Admiral Dewey and a reminder of the *Maine*. General Nelson Miles came home from the wars to the nearby town of Westminster, and his red face with the heavy white handle-bar mustache was a common sight to school children, who found it hard to believe that this slow-moving old gentleman had fought the wild Apaches of the West. Teddy Roosevelt once drove down Main Street in an open brougham, smiling his famous smile . . . At the time these were intangibles—exciting but without significance. Only in retrospect can one detect the pattern of the times that overlay those days of youth.

A feeling of permanence pervaded everything. Perhaps it was just childhood that made it so. But when you grow up and go through the school years in the town where you were born, there is a continuity of existence that gives you the sense of a world destined to go on forever. Policeman Young, sunning himself in front of City Hall in a white helmet, his big stomach protruding, couldn't have chased a robber. He was too fat and too indolent. But to us he meant law and order. It took me many years to believe seriously that policemen could be as venial as other men. In those days they were a class apart. As was the dread Black Maria, its rear grimly curtained to shield its inmates in off-prohibition years. The solid granite Court House personified Justice, so much so that years later when I read James Gould Cozzens' novel of the law, *By Love Possessed*, I visualized its enactment entirely around Monument Square and the old Court House. The jail was out of the way, in South Fitchburg. One gave it little thought—only a shadow of a shudder as you passed it in the trolley.

.   .   .

Fitchburg was not just a commonplace middle-class town. It wasn't so much of a city that you couldn't be in the country twenty minutes from the Common. Climb Flat Rock Hill and you had a view of the town below you and Wachusett Mountain beyond. Ride your bike toward Lunenburg and you were in placid rolling farm land. Out Mechanic Street way the roadside was white and pink with laurel in June, and earlier still you could find mayflowers on the same road. You had to know their hidden place and scratch under last fall's brown leaves, sometimes even a patch of snow, to find them. But there they'd be, hardy little pale-pink blossoms with the loveliest smell of any flower that grows. I see them in New York sometimes in the florist shop, a tiny bunch already rusty, but with that unbelievable, unforgettable fragrance.

Beyond Fitchburg to the north the hills were covered with farms, but as I was growing up, not entirely Yankee farms. Hard-working Finns were taking them over, finding in that stony unyielding country the kind of land they knew best. From their hilltops the view was true New England —old rounded mountains covered with rocky pastures and clumps of evergreen, and in the valleys a few small villages.

Ashby and New Ipswich were two of those villages. They lay on the border of Massachusetts and New Hampshire in the shadow of Mount Watatic, a small unassuming mountain with a two-pronged summit, little known and well off the beaten path. Ashby and New Ipswich themselves have always been out-of-the-way villages, never quaint enough to lure tourists, their people farmers for a hundred and fifty years and, before that, lumbermen.

On the lower slope of Mount Watatic, near its foot, lies a cellar hole which everyone in the region knows as "the old Whitney place." Weeds have grown around the granite-stone foundation, but in the space around the cellar hole, where trees and bushes have not entirely encroached, the contour of a farm remains. A very old man in New Ipswich told me as late as 1935 that he remembered buildings on the Whitney farm when he was a boy.

It was here that my grandfather John Whitney was born, and his father John before him. Josiah, my grandfather's grandfather, brought his bride there from Watertown in 1799. He built the Watatic homestead, cut down the primeval forest and cleared away the glacial deposits for his plow, as the sturdy stone walls still standing bear witness.

I remember my grandfather distinctly even though he died before I began to go to school—very tall, with a beard and kind eyes. His name was John Cushing Whitney but he was known to all as "Cush." Everyone liked Cush Whitney, the old man from New Ipswich told me, "a fine-looking, hard-working, genial man." On Sunday mornings he would take my hand and we'd walk down Main Street in Fitchburg to get the Sunday paper. At the paper store he'd buy me a bag of candy, a small paper bag striped red and green. Even at that undiscriminating age I didn't like the candy, but I was proud to carry the bag. My mother, born in New Ipswich, was his middle daughter Ida, whom he called his "curly-head." There was a deep bond between those two which I in my turn shared and which probably molded my young life into its predominantly Yankee cast.

In his young days my grandfather had a sawmill, a remnant of which is still there. I saw it one lovely spring day not long ago. He was a lumberman and sometimes went as far afield as Virginia to act as a tree consultant. Curiously enough, this knowledgableness of wood was part of the family history. The early Whitneys were carpenters, and the later ones, organ builders.

Out of trees, wood; out of wood, organs; out of organs, a good ear; and out of a good ear, music. Jonas Whitney was an organ builder; his grandson became an organist and composer; and the next generation were singers. Myron Whitney was the great American basso of the sixties and seventies, and his son William taught voice to pupils ranging from Louise Homer to Eleanor Steber.

I linger on this musical bypath with special fondness because my own children, remote though they were from Myron and William, were both born with perfect pitch, and also because of the fancy that perhaps it all goes back to the singing Welsh near whose border their ancestors as well as my children's ancestors were born. I have seen the beautiful green country in the Wye valley where they came from. There is a village of Whitney to this day, and Merbach Hill rises above Whitney Wood. This is close to Wales, and Whitneys of all branches, whether humble or eminent in later American circles, still have the wide face and rather heavy features of the Welsh, black hair, and eyes with heavy brows.

Mary Pillsbury, also of Ashby, was my grandmother. I guess the Whitneys were a cut above the Pillsburys in England. William, their progenitor in this country, came over in 1641 to escape the consequences of a misdemeanor: he was admonished for "lack of decorum in romance," and hired himself out as a servant in Boston to pay for his passage.

There was nothing romantic about the Pillsburys by the time I knew them. Often of a Sunday my parents used to drive in a surrey the ten miles out from Fitchburg to Ashby to visit Uncle Charles Pillsbury, with me, their only child, on the back seat, grumpy on the way out, and on the home trip in the dark of evening, sound asleep.

The Pillsbury farmhouse I remember well. It was

built by my great-grandfather of bricks made on the place, and still stands, as solid as when it was new, with the great-great-grandchildren still carrying on. In the outside kitchen there was a soapstone sink with pump, and a tin basin in which we washed our hands. The big table around which we ate could take an indefinite number of relatives, and the food I recall vividly as boiled chicken with well-seasoned gravy, sponge cake so light it could float away, and good cold milk which in that day of no refrigeration must have been kept in the well. Aunt Lucy, Charles's wife, with red cheeks and bright blue eyes, looked like the picture of Cezanne's wife—with hands folded on her stomach.

There was no drama in the story of the Whitneys and the Pillsburys. The fact that both families settled in Ashby is of importance to practically no one. But it remains one of the anomalies of human nature. Knowing the labor and patience that were needed a hundred and fifty years ago to shape that little village out of the stony New England hillside, one wonders. Why, of all places, Ashby?

While Cush Whitney and Benjamin Pillsbury were both growing up in the security of a decent Puritan community, a young Irish lad named Daniel Kielty was starving in County Mayo, Ireland. The overseer of an English lord had evicted his father and family from the small cabin which was their home, as he and other overseers evicted thousands of other Irish peasants, so that the vast estates could be turned into rolling fields of crops and cattle. Lest the poor tenants try to return—as many did—a crowbar brigade pounded down the roofs of the cabins, but Daniel's father was made of sterner stuff. Instead of turning back he sought out a spot in the bog—the Bad Lands that nobody wanted—and with a creel of sod on his back he built up a new home for his family. Back and forth, in and out, with nothing but his back and his two hands, he made first a "boreen," a little roadway into the bog, then pounded in enough solid earth to hold a cabin, and another patch of ground on which to grow potatoes. I have seen the spot of emerald green in the bog, and the walls of the cabin, long deserted.

What happened everybody knows. In 1846, in December, a blight fell upon the potatoes. A whole crop was ruined, and the next year a second crop. Potatoes were the only food that the Irish peasants had, and now they were dying of starvation and disease. Whole villages disappeared. Mayo of all the counties was the worst hit. "Mayo-God-help-us!" in Irish parlance still means rock bottom in misery. Those who had the strength crept along the roadside to Castlebar, the capital of Mayo, to beg for food. And some were lucky enough—through money sent over by the Irish in other lands—to get passage on ships to Australia, and Canada, and the United States. But an incredible number were still to die on the terrible voyage across the Atlantic.

Daniel Kielty, with his parents and sisters, survived. They landed in Boston, and eventually, by way of a five-cent fare to Cambridge by train, and stagecoach from Cambridge on, Daniel himself reached Fitchburg. There he married Bridget Moran of Westport, Ireland, and raised a family of six children. In 1864 he became a soldier in the Union Army, and after three months in the Army and one hour on the battlefield, was killed in the Battle of the Wilderness. It is a short and tragic story—the life of my grandfather Kielty.

While the poor Kieltys were starving in Ireland, the Whitneys and the Pillsburys were secure and respected citizens of a real democracy, bringing up their children in a God-fearing community. By the time the Kieltys were straining their weakened bodies to reach the New World, the others had been settled in for two hundred years. And as fate had brought the two Anglo-Saxon clans together and united them in Ashby, so it was in the stars that their offspring should come face to face with the Irish Kieltys in Fitchburg.

By rights I should have been the psychiatrist's delight —child of a mixed marriage and an only child to boot, thrown into the maelstrom of notorious Yankee-Irish antipathy.

My father was an Irish Catholic, my mother a Yankee Protestant descendant of Puritan settlers. They may both have been exceptions to their kind. But I'm inclined to think that by my time the sharp edge of Yankee intolerance had been worn smoother in provincial Fitchburg than in Boston where politics kept it alive; also that the Irish in this smaller community had themselves become Yankees.

It must have been looks that first drew Tom Kielty and Ida Whitney together. "I always liked to see your father and mother walking downstreet together!" a woman said to me years later, savoring the recollection appreciatively. "They were such a handsome couple!"

"Cush Whitney's three daughters were all smart, and all good-looking," the old man from New Ipswich told me who knew my grandfather. "And Tom Kielty was a handsome fellow."

Handsome he was indeed—six foot two, with a straight back and an erect carriage. He walked well. And a whole generation of elderly people still live in Fitchburg who remember him as Drum Major Kielty, marching down Main Street at the head of the Fitchburg Military Band in Fourth of July and Decoration Day parades. No twirling or throwing the stick in the air in those days, just the dignified right-to-left, even beat with a big heavy round-headed baton.

I have pictures of both my parents taken the year they became engaged. My mother was sixteen, and my father nine years older. The pictures were taken at Moulton's, the best photography studio in town, probably on the same day. Size and arrangement are identical. The young man on the stiff cardboard has his hair combed with crisp precision, and his stylishly large mustache ever so slightly waxed at the ends. A stickpin in his cravat indicates the elegance with which he wished to be presented. He is the barber's and tailor's Beau Brummell of the 1890's, as is practically every young man of that day who has come down to us by photograph.

On the other hand, in spite of the blandness of the photographer's art, my mother comes through with personality. The face is oval, and the mouth, well shaped and untarnished by lipstick, is lovely. The curled fringe on her forehead is as precise as her fiancé's mustache. A lace scarf around her neck is tightly folded to her figure, over what seems to be a black poplin dress. And the touch of narrow white collar above the black looks chic even now. She obviously had a sense of style. But it is the eyes that catch you, not so large, but shining-bright, and to me, perceptive and very appealing.

They must have been very much in love. Those shining eyes may have meant the defiance of a girl who was going to live her life in her own way. But this was no runaway elopement. Ida and Tom were engaged a conservative five years, perhaps as a concession to Ida's family. She was very young; she *might change her mind*. But she didn't . . .

My father was not the typical Irishman, not witty or

debonair. He worked steadily at his modest business, and his pleasures were of the simplest. What he liked even better than leading the band was to fish in Wachusett Lake. He used to catch pout (not trout!), a fish I have never encountered since those days. For some reason it could be angled for only after dark, and, fried for dinner the next day, it made the best fish dish I have ever known. It was he who found the mayflowers in early spring. He'd go out while the snow was still in the woods, and when I was a big girl and away at college, he always sent me a shoebox full, packed in wet moss.

Before my time he had been a first-class baseball player. I learned this only after I was married and chanced to meet an old-timer from Fitchburg at a World Series game in New York. He said that my father had been an outstanding pitcher, and could have been a pro if he'd really put his mind to it.

That opened vistas to me. How would my mother have liked it if my father had been a Big Leaguer? Brought up in respectable Ashby and New Ipswich, she might momentarily have found it a hurdle, but I am certain she would have loved the life of movement and excitement. I always felt that my mother longed for larger fields. She went to poetry readings at the Woman's Club and to the Edward Howard Griggs lectures, enormously popular with the ladies in those days. She took me to song recitals in Symphony Hall in Boston, where I remember we heard Sembrich and Nordica. She had an appreciation of the world of culture without any first-hand knowledge of it. Much too early she lost her youthful slenderness, and her curly hair turned gray. When I was in college she sometimes sent me a fudge cake in my laundry, as my father sent me arbutus, and she made all my dresses. She was a good cook and a fine needlewoman.

All in all, they were an ordinary couple of ordinary means in an ordinary town, with a little girl to bring up. They gave me what I look back on as a very happy childhood. By the actual nature of their union—the mingling of religions and traditions—they bridged the rift to my great advantage. I never knew what bigotry was.

They brought me up a Catholic. I went to Mass on Sunday and ate fish on Friday. But I grew up a Yankee. I fell into line with Protestant Fitchburg more than with the Irish Catholics. My mother became a Catholic—a good Catholic!—but she did not become Irish, and I think the Irish felt slightly alien toward her, particularly my father's unmarried sisters. This was no problem that I know of for my father, who was completely with his wife on every issue. But the Irish Kielty "girls" may have thought they had reason to worry. Both their brothers married out of the Church, as later their only three nieces, all of whom had long happy lives with their non-Catholic husbands.

The Whitneys, who had no son, took my father to their hearts. They made him heir to my grandfather's small coal business, and the relationship between my grandmother's household and ours was warm and intimate.

Occasionally I went with her to the C. C. Church (Calvinistic Congregational), and sat in the second pew, where I was slightly more bored than at St. Bernard's where I had already that morning attended the children's early Mass. It was not with evangelical intent that my grandmother took me there, and certainly with no bitterness in her soul. Probably she liked to have her only available grandchild with her, and on these particular Sundays she may have been baby-sitting—an unheard-of term then, and still unknown when my own children needed it, but by whatever name, a pastime of grandmothers.

My parents both died while I was in my early twenties

—my father first, and my mother when she was only forty-seven. When I think of her now it is the middle-aged woman I see, and in her eyes, not the shining brightness of that early picture but the shadow of sadness. Life had more to offer than she would ever attain. And the irony was that almost immediately after her death her own child was plunged headlong into that world of variety and excitement that her mother had sensed but never encountered. The daughter swam about awkwardly at first, but gradually with ease, in waters that soon became familiar.

I believe that the people in Fitchburg in those years were quite without the taint of intolerance. There was, to be sure, the same precise demarkation between Protestants and Catholics, as there was between the rich and the poor. But no one got worked up. We heard about bigotry in distant places—the A.P.A., for one. What those initials stood for I didn't know (American Protective Association). I only knew that it was against Catholics. But as far as Fitchburg was concerned, the A.P.A. was as remote as the Spanish Inquisition.

There was only one colored family in town. They were highly respected workpeople who lived in a shack which the trolley passed on the way to Whalom. It had a little yard and a tall sunflower beside the door, and was close to a grove of trees where gypsies sometimes camped during the summer. Gypsies we were afraid of. But the colored people were like all the other working people of the town. I recall the mother of the family sitting in our kitchen having a cup of tea with my mother after she had helped with the ironing.

My knowledge of Jews was very limited. There were a few Jewish families down on Boutelle Street near the Catholic cemetery. The junk dealer, who drove a dilapidated wagon with a clanging bell, lived there. And I recall a slight feeling of uneasiness when I passed through that street because of the unknown element. I had heard there were only Jews living there and I didn't know any Jews. Or thought I didn't. Actually I knew several Jews, I realize on looking back, but they didn't live on Boutelle Street. Two or three were in my class at school, and one was among my closest friends. I don't know that they would have designated themselves as Jews. The subject never came up and nothing in any way ever differentiated them from the other children.

I don't know what the connotations of such a town may be to outsiders. An actor told me that when the name "Fitchburg" came up, as it did in a play in which he was acting, Boston audiences always laughed, the way Broadway audiences laugh at the mention of Brooklyn. Being on the inside, I still have no idea why it should be so about Fitchburg. Maybe it was an "innocent" town. Or maybe my memories have bathed it in my own innocence.

Half a century after these times that I have been recalling, I went back to this corner of New England. Everything had happened to the world in that time. And much to me.

I drove slowly, alone, out to Ashby from Fitchburg. So many of the houses on Mechanic Street were the same! The Finns were still at the north end, as they had been. There was a steam bath advertised. And the curves in the ten-mile road were familiar.

Before I got to Ashby I turned off on South Valley Road, and drove three miles down it on good hard dirt, with trees meeting overhead and a stream rushing along beside me. That was where I came upon the millpond, with a shed still standing, where my grandfather Whitney's old saw-mill had been operating in the 1860's. In all the three miles I didn't meet a car or see a person.

Just over the border in New Hampshire, in New Ipswich, I saw the farmhouse under the two still healthy, tall elm trees where my mother was born. I saw Uncle Charles's sturdy brick house and the hills sloping away from it. It was facing Mount Watatic broadside. And driving as far as I could over a rough, rutted path I finally got out on the lower mountainside and walked up to the old Whitney cellar hole. I sat down. It was late afternoon and the sun had warmed the stones on which I sat. There was the open space of the farmyard around me and not far off blueberry bushes and pine trees—the essence of New England fragrance. I could see other wooded hills, but no houses.

In the cemetery not far from the mountain, I walked from stone to stone. They were all there: Whitneys, Jaquiths, Wellingtons, Pillsburys, Damons, Marbles—all relatives. At one end there were newer graves. That was where the Finns were buried—in a countryside so much like their own.

The center of Ashby was a dream come true. After fifty years, not a change. Not a new house. The handsome Unitarian Church dominated the small Common, the gold hands of its fine four-faced clock shining. The Congregational Church, only slightly less beautiful, stood on the other side of the Common, at right angles. Opposite it, the inn looked the same, a long yellow tavern-like building with a swinging sign, but it was no longer used as a hostelry. The one store still had its narrow porch, two steps up, and overhang. But when I went in I found big modern freezers, well stocked. Ashby isn't outlandish. It is just pleasantly conservative.

New Ipswich village, always richer than Ashby, looked as I remembered it, with a row of really beautiful white houses well set on green lawns under big trees.

I didn't see a supermarket or a service station or a development in either of these townships.

But Fitchburg was something else. Here modernity had laid its plain practical hand on most of Main Street. The old buildings, unassuming and not good-looking to start with, still stand, but are now trimmed with glass extensions, bay windows, bulging excrescenses—an architect's nightmare. This is true not only of Fitchburg, of course, but all towns of any size.

Once off Main Street the past came back fitfully. I walked over to the house where I was born, now so much closer to the house next door than my three-year-old eyes had seen it, and went past my grandmother Kielty's house on the same street. The house where my Whitney grandparents lived is still standing, plain dark-red city brick— but with the falsest of false fronts. It is on Main Street.

In Fitchburg my heart did not lift until I got to the Catholic cemetery.

All my life the consciousness of the Watatic Whitneys had been a part of me. Through them I had somehow bridged the distance from 1799 to the mid-twentieth century in a smooth arc. What surprised me in St. Bernard's cemetery was that I now felt for the first time a part of the Kielty clan as well. When I revisited St. Bernard's, something quite unexpected happened: the whole lively talkative good-looking Irish world of Fitchburg came alive as if by magic. There lay May Roddy among all her brothers and sisters. May Roddy had taken me to school, and I remember the pointed toes of her shoes. The McAuliffe shaft of granite: of course a granite shaft, because the McAuliffes had quarried a third of Rollstone Hill. The Burkes— Major Burke! What had he been a major of? The Lennon relatives

I'd almost forgotten; J. R. Smith, the undertaker, always known familiarly as "J.R.," the Careys who used to wave to me when they passed our house before I was five; the O'Tooles; the McCartys.

There is nothing sad about an Irish cemetery. Death does not terrify the Irish. They have lived close to it through so many generations. Wakes are parties. Folks look forward to them. "I'll be the next," one says, and sure enough, someone else notes later, she was. In those earlier days that I am remembering, death came lingeringly. Perhaps I am thinking of the tuberculosis cases that were so frequent. I can remember hearing about family and friends filing into the bedroom to say goodbye, as if the sick one were leaving for the Old Country. Unlike Watatic cemetery where the thunder of Jehovah might be heard behind the mountain, St. Bernard's was an altogether cheerful rendezvous.

After I left St. Bernard's I walked along Boutelle Street. And sure enough, after fifty years, there was a kosher sign on a shop. And a small synagogue. The chief difference was that I felt very much at home.

❁ *Part Two* ❁

THE CITY

NEW YORK WITH
CREAM—1908

In my Fitchburg days New York had little attraction for
the young. To them and to New Englanders in general New
York was unrefined. It was "loud"—a dubious region over
which hung ominous shadows unknown in our sunny skies.

The shooting of Stanford White on the roof of Madison Square Garden sent an electric shock across the country. The Fitchburg *Sentinel* ran it with censorial brevity,
but the Boston *Globe*, to which nearly everyone in town
subscribed, withheld none of the melodramatic detail. This
spectacular crime of passion was said to have had a morbid
fascination for young girls, who now couldn't wait to get
to New York. Every young thing saw herself as a potential
Evelyn Nesbit, chorus girl and artist's model, long hair
hanging down in a curl over her shoulder, and with rich

lover and great artist fighting for her favor. The lurid disclosure of the court trial only whetted their appetites for the giddy whirlpool of life.

Apparently I was too young to find this drama alluring. My own romantic yearnings were blissfully satisfied with school dances and all their joyous appurtenances— fluffy dresses and long gloves, dance orders with pencil dangling, initials which quickened the heartbeat. The intricate steps of the schottische were a challenge met only by the best dancers (of whom I believe I was one), and the waltz was dreamiest just when the orchestra began softly playing "Goodnight Ladies": twelve o'clock had struck and a never-to-be-forgotten evening had come to a close . . .

I was still in this artless stage when New York burst upon me full-blown. It was a stereopticon view, every object and scene standing forth detached and vivid and throbbingly alive, even though completely apart from my own personal life. The year was 1908, I had been but a few brief months in college, and now found myself spending a joyous week with my roommate who came from New York.

On our green campus I had taken this roommate for granted. We were friends. She borrowed from me as I borrowed from her. We were both anonymous and inconspicuous in the leveling way of school, and indistinguishable from all our other friendly companions. But against her family background, as I saw when I visited her, she was far from anonymous.

The family itself was a revelation. These were people a world apart from the one I had been brought up in, distinguished by achievement and wealth, and in my consciousness haloed with a radiance that has never lost its glow. Through all the years that have now passed since that Elysian week, I have never forgotten the very special flavor of that remarkable group of people.

The father of the family, Samuel Weiss, was one of
New York's foremost corporation lawyers——a man of domi-
nant personality who never sidestepped an issue however
trifling, and who ruled his family, not with a regulation
iron rod but with the scales of justice in one hand balanced
somewhat unevenly against the precepts of his own strongly
held beliefs. The subtle but unmistakable distinction that
emanated from that family, for which I believe he was
solely responsible, was their separateness. Mr. Weiss es-
chewed popular resorts for his children: no Long Branch,
Deal, Poland Springs or Catskill mountains for them, but
a rustic lodge on one of the most distant and least populated
of the Maine lakes. He refused to have an automobile at a
time when automobiles were still noisy and unreliable. Instead of a mansion on Fifth Avenue, which he could well
have afforded, he chose the unfashionable magnificence of
the Hudson. There must be no show, no pretense, no vulgarity——in a day when show and pretense and vulgarity
were the criteria of worldly success. It was a demand for
moderation made by one whom his children sometimes considered the most immoderate of men. Much was given them,
and much was expected from them in the way of sharpened
perceptions, sound judgment, integrity.

By the time I knew him he was a heavy man with
pointed beard and sharp eyes, a nineteenth-century figure
of larger-than-life proportions. He had a friend and crony
who portrayed even more vividly the storybook world so
far removed from Fitchburg. He was a cosmopolite, as
much at home in the capitals of Europe as in New York,
cultivated, elliptical of speech, fastidiously groomed. The
two old gentlemen——they had probably just about turned
fifty——drank long whisky-sodas at dinner; after dinner, in
a mass of heavy cigar smoke, they played pinochle in the
library, surrounded by the dark red-brown leather of law
books. I recall the card table as if it were yesterday, with

the strong short-fingered hands upon it, which the desk lamp lighted with theatrical brightness. Theirs was a masculine world.

My roommate's two brothers were lawyers-to-be. Billy, the elder, was at Yale, planning to enter his father's firm, as he eventually did; and Louis was in knee pants— in a day when pre-college boys still did wear short pants. Even their little sister Carol, only a child then, went into law. The only non-lawyer was my friend Nina, who ended up marrying a lawyer.

And her mother. Mrs. Weiss was a small woman of modest beauty. She was one of seven children of a big department-store dynasty, all but one married by my time, and nearly all living in New York. There was Aunt Zilla and Aunt Frankie, and Aunt Florence and Aunt Min, and the uncles with their cigars. As an only child I looked with wonder on this group of New York matrons when they gathered in their sister's upstairs sitting room, all in dark silk dresses and hats and gloves, gossiping, talking, laughing. They all had fine well-run homes to which we were invited in turn during my golden week, but none had the air of the house on the Hudson. None had a masculine influence of quite such powerful proportions.

If the mother of the house was quietly assured, it is not to be wondered at. She had everything. She didn't say much in the gathering of her immediate family. They didn't give her an opening. But she had much to offer a young girl visitor.

All the others were highly articulate and constantly engaged in good-natured argument that no doubt kept them in fine professional trim. The give-and-take of those family conversations ranks high in my recollections. There was a grace of speech and a turn of fancy among the Weisses that made table talk elsewhere and ever since seem stale and airless. Even their handwriting is artistic and original, much alike, with easily identifiable hallmarks.

The beautiful home in which this family was so strongly entrenched was a large square brick house on 180th Street high over the Hudson. The brick was painted white with a trim of chocolate brown. It was surrounded by sloping lawns, and had a lilac hedge, a vegetable garden and a panoramic view of the river for miles. To reach it we took the subway to 168th Street. There we were met by a carriage and driven the mile or so to the house on the heights. We could have continued on the subway to 181st Street, but contrary to the ways of present-day New Yorkers, the Weisses liked the slow approach. Our drive north, parallel to the Hudson, was in a low-seated brougham with the accompanying clink of horses' hoofs on stone pavement.

The house was on the slope of the Fort Washington hill, the summit of which, now covered by the Cloisters, was then dominated by the mansion and stables of Mr. C. K. G. Billings. Nearby Libby Castle, with turrets and formidable, thick walls, had been the home of Boss William Tweed, but when I was there, was occupied by close friends of my hostess. Down the hill a little lived Wallingford Riegger, the composer, also a neighborhood friend, and a few blocks farther east, George Grey Barnard, the sculptor.

The New York that I looked upon from this rare vantage point was a stage curtain of strong colors and gleaming textures. Vistas were foreshortened and figures and structures stylized—a fantastic promise of even more fascination once the rich folds were drawn aside. I had no comprehension whatsoever of the city's gigantic size or its intricate make-up. But I do recall distinctly the streets through which we walked and drove during that memorable week, and the buildings we passed; I recollect how the sun shone and the people smiled. And to know with precision in 1964 how even a few bright corners of New York looked in 1908 seems to me a matter for wonder and gratitude.

Grand Central Station, where we arrived by train from Boston, was just being built. Its gold marble interior was not finished. Its exits and entrances for passengers were boardwalks and narrow wooden corridors (and remained so for years). Trains came into the station on open tracks that ran along Park Avenue, at that time as likely a pathway for future elegance as any railroad-switching area on the Boston & Maine.

The subway was quite new, I have learned since, having been opened with great ceremony only in 1904. It was a single line, running south to Atlantic Avenue, Brooklyn, and north on the West Side to Van Cortland. A baseball park faced the 168th Street station where we got off, occupying the ground on which the Medical Center now stands. This was the home field of the Highlanders, predecessors to the Yankees. Times Square was only a local stop on the subway. Theater-goers from uptown had a neat decision to make: to change from the express at Seventy-Second and make three extra stops, or swoop down to Grand Central and take the local back one station. Manhattan East-Siders, such as they were—Germans from Yorkville, and Irish from many settlements along the way—had to use the El to get downtown fast.

The Public Library at Forty-Second Street was nearly finished. In its pure whiteness and classical dignity I thought it the most beautiful building I had ever seen, but at the Weiss dinner table I learned that there could be differences of opinion upon matters esthetic. Billy and his college friends attacked the architecture of the new building, as we might nowadays question a Lever Brothers crea-

tion of glass or condemn a Guggenheim Museum. But let
it be said quickly for the perspicacity of those young 1908
critics that they found its Carrera and Hastings architecture not too radical, but already too traditional.

Mrs. Weiss had no opinions on architecture, but she
did speak wistfully of the reservoir which had been filled in
behind the library to make what is now Bryant Park. That
was the spot where she and her husband had become engaged, walking around it one evening at sunset (as I, in
turn, was to become engaged several years later in front of
the right lion on the library steps, shortly after nightfall).

It was Eastertime, with New York at its most resplendent. On Easter Sunday we heard High Mass in St.
Patrick's towering cathedral, seated close to the altar rail
on the right of the center aisle. This was the old Tweed
pew, hospitably offered this non-Catholic family because of
their Catholic visitor.

Fifth Avenue was decorous, and we strolled through
the fashionable crowd with wondrous ease. The hats were
Merry Widows that year, wide of brim and wreathed
with flowers. They sat high on the head, pinned fast to
solid pompadours in front and Psyche knots behind.
Dresses were long sheath gowns slit to the knee, the better
for strolling. And the men who have survived in my memory wore high silk hats which they doffed often and with
ceremony on that sunny Sunday noon.

On Easter Saturday *Tannhäuser* was sung at the Metropolitan Opera House, and there we were in the red plush
magnificence of the diamond horseshoe, deep in orchestra
seats, tiers upon tiers of balconies rising above us, and before us the curtain of gold. I shall never forget the nerve-
tingling hush when the orchestra struck up its opening
chords, or the smothered acclaim as the curtain swayed
slowly back to disclose the maze and mists of Venusberg,

the dim figures of dancing handmaidens, and Venus herself reclining on a cloud—the chiffon-draped, sturdy figure of Olive Fremstad in her prime.

In those days there were not many restaurants where the young daughters of respectable families were allowed to go. But one evening we were taken to the Plaza Hotel for dinner. The Plaza had just opened (though I didn't know it until 1958 when I read of its fiftieth anniversary) and a dazzling spectacle it was. I know the Plaza still and like to go there above all other hotels, but in my memory's eye it was of an elegance then which has somewhat paled, though not too much, with time. The rugs can't be so rich as they were then, nor the chandeliers with all their prismatic brilliance quite so glittering. The long marble corridors have shortened perceptibly, and gone forever are the gentlemen in evening capes.

Across from the Plaza was the Hotel Netherlands with a narrow piazza along its front, where gentlemen sat and ogled the passing crowd. This was not for us—nor the Knickerbocker Hotel, which we passed when we went to the Opera. This was strictly taboo. It had the original King Cole Bar, I was to learn later, and was the home of Caruso and many another famous singer. The Astor nearby was also out of bounds. Its lobby, we were told, was a rendezvous for sightseers.

We did go to Maillard's restaurant on Twenty-sixth Street, diagonally across Fifth Avenue from the still aristocratic Holland House. There we had hot chocolate after visiting Altman's new store at Thirty-fourth Street. It was a sad day for the prestige of Jordan & Marsh of Washington Street, Boston, even of R. H. Stearns of Tremont Street, when I saw Altman's.

Polly of the Circus, with Mabel Taliaferro, was our play. And around the piano in the house on Fort Washington, we were singing "The Saucy Little Bird on Nellie's Hat," "Glow-Worm," and "H-A-double-R-I, G-A-N spells Harrigan." The house was lively with boys and girls, invited no doubt for the guest's entertainment, and countless friendly aunts and uncles. It was a week gay beyond belief.

That was the New York of 1908, seen through a gilded keyhole. A shining view, and utterly misleading.

III

STARVING NEW YORK

Another New York, which filtered more gradually into my experience and left a deeper impact, I can describe only by marshaling together some of the outside facts and figures that created it.

It was the glittering surface of New York that I saw in 1908 from the luxurious home on the slope of Fort Washington. Of the monster writhing below the surface I knew nothing. That three-quarters of this magnificent city was half starved and living in unspeakable filth would have been as inconceivable to me as doubtless to most of the chocolate drinkers in Maillard's or the Easter Day Fifth Avenue strollers. Had anyone told them that the most concentrated poverty in the world lay right there, in a few dozen blocks of their own city, many of them would have dismissed it as melodrama. Yet every week from 1905 on, tens of thousands of people were dumped onto the New York docks from immigrant ships—pale, sick, homeless, frightened people—while the contented citizens of the uptown West Side continued to pursue their even course in blissful indifference.

It would take a major catastrophe to open their eyes. And on March 8, 1911, that catastrophe occurred—a tragedy of such devastating horror that the city was brought to a momentary standstill. This was the Triangle Shirtwaist factory fire in which a hundred and forty-six workers were trapped and burned to death—mostly young girls.

The Triangle factory occupied the top three floors of a building on Greene Street, just east of Washington Square. The fire started around four-thirty on a clear cold Saturday afternoon, just as the operators were preparing to go home —early, because it was Saturday. Just how the fire started was never wholly established, but it spread with lightning speed, catching up the flimsy material of shirtwaists and blowing it in clouds of flame through the draughty open lofts. The workers rushed from fire escape to elevator to stairway, screaming in panic. But all outlets of escape were quickly blocked. The fire escape, bent by the heat and the weight of the struggling mass of bodies, buckled in and dumped its load into the yard below where a crowd, already gathered, looked on in speechless horror. The elevators, with two valiant operators, carried all they could until they too collapsed. Exit doors opened in instead of out. One door on the sixth floor was locked.

The first fire alarm was turned in at four forty-five and at five o'clock ten thousand people had surrounded the building. Most of the workers came from poor Jewish and Italian homes in the neighboring slums, and now thousands of their relatives poured into the open spaces of Washington Square Park, the police trying in vain to hold them back. They surged toward the burning building. Fire and smoke were belching from the top-story windows. Girls could be seen clinging to the window ledges, and the crowd yelled to them to hang on. But frantic with fear they jumped, one after another, the fire roaring behind them, their hair and dresses aflame.

Incredible as it seems, the fire was put out in exactly eighteen minutes. But the agony increased as the terrible search for bodies began. At six o'clock Chief Croker of the Fire Department worked his way into the three top floors of the building. Through the still drifting smoke he saw bodies burned to bare bones. "Skeletons bending over sewing-machines," he said later on the witness stand. (The final word on the fire and the ensuing trial has been written in Leon Stein's admirable book, *The Triangle Fire*.)

Firemen had to lower the bodies to the ground by block and tackle, with a man stationed at each floor to reach out and push the corpses clear of the sills. By six forty-five it was dark, and searchlights picked out the ghoulish objects swinging along the side of the building. As each body neared the ground and the police reached up for it, a moan rose from the watching men and women.

The police had sent for one hundred coffins but the morgue could supply only sixty-five, and the charred bodies, wet from fire hoses, lay on the sidewalk where they were carefully—tenderly—covered by tarpaulin. The morgue itself was too small to hold them all, and a roofed pier at the foot of East Twenty-third Street was converted into a temporary resting place. Slowly the wagons with their dead drove up through the silent, crowded streets, up Broadway to Fourteenth Street, over to Third Avenue and across Twenty-third, their bells clanging.

When volunteers were called on to help, twenty-four

derelicts came from Bowery flophouses and offered their services. But the horror of it was so intense that the crews had to be completely changed three times during the night. All day Sunday the living walked through the aisles of coffins trying to identify the dead. Two hundred thousand persons made their way to the pier.

One week after the fire, of the one hundred and forty-six dead, only seven remained without names.

The sensational details made an indelible impression on New York's social conscience. What is now a chapter in social science textbooks was then living history. The workers in the Triangle factory came from that nameless mass of immigrants that had been piling into New York for the previous six years. And now, through the flames of that tragedy, old settled New Yorkers became aware, for the first time, of their poverty, of the dangerous conditions under which they had to work, of their great number.

And the number grew.

It was like the homeless Irish who had been cast out of western Ireland in the 1840's and made their way to the New World. Now the helpless and starving of central Europe, in far greater numbers, were forced westward by much the same kind of economic conditions. And the powers-that-be were glad to see the last of them. On the Continent, as in Ireland, the old order was changing. Land was concentrated into fewer and larger estates, and big-scale agriculture left no place for small peasant-holdings. In the way of all European peasantry these people lived, not on isolated farms as in America but together in villages, trudging out to their fields each day. And now that the fields were lost the villages in turn became poorer—and poorer. Hardest hit of all were the Jews who were small shopkeepers in the villages, the middlemen who could no longer make a living, and upon whom the peasants, true to historic tradition, now vented their impotent wrath. It was the day of pogroms and organized massacres to which the governments, particularly that of Russia, closed their eyes.

Nothing was left for the Jews of eastern Europe but escape. Sometimes on foot, sometimes by cart, for some lucky ones by railroad, they made their way from town to town, from border to border, across Europe to the seaports of the Atlantic. Other Jews already settled in America helped them, as the Irish had helped their own a generation earlier. From 1905 on, during the nine years before the war of 1914, one and a quarter million Old World Jews, one-seventh of all the Jews in Europe, left.

According to the book, the percentages of Jews who emigrated to the United States in those years was the same as that of general emigration during that period from eastern Europe. But as the majority of Jews who left Europe ended their wandering when they reached New York, they became an essential part of the New York story. And of my story.

They made their homes in New York—if you can call it "making a home" to live in the muck and dirt of the Rivington Street, Division Street, Orchard, Hester, Baxter streets of that day. The Lower East Side had long been the burrowing hole for the poorest of the city's population. Five Points and the notorious Bend of Mulberry Street had first been hiding places for escaped English criminals, after them the Irish poor, then the Germans. Now it was the eastern Europeans, and of them in the largest number, the Jews.

Land was scarce and time was urgent. Top-heavy tenements were hastily erected in this already crowded section, buildings six to eight stories high—from one to three hundred people huddled together on a plot of ground that measured twenty by a hundred feet.

Sanitary conditions were unspeakable—sometimes there was one toilet to a building, at best one to a floor, and that in the hallway, the property of all, tended by none, filthy and stinking. Bitter cold swept through the cold-water flats in winter; and the sweaty heat of summer was if anything worse. Epidemics flourished.

This was the American ghetto, miserable, crowded, poverty-stricken. Yet not entirely grim.

The Jews were at least together, and safe. They had a nesting colony. In time they became almost a city in themselves, with a Yiddish newspaper, a Jewish theater, kosher butchers, synagogues, Hebrew schools.

Every day but Saturday the ghetto was a beehive, a mass of constantly moving people, a medley of perpetual city noises. Vendors called and buyers argued. Children screamed and their mothers shouted. Pushcarts with food lined Orchard and Hester streets—bread, meat, fish. On Grand Street, rivaling the stores, were the pushcarts that sold notions, drygoods, wearing apparel.

On hot nights women sat on the high steps of the tenements trying to catch a breeze. They wore *sheitls*, those ugly unnatural wigs that Orthodox Jewish women don after marriage. To the passer-by they looked all alike and all unattractive, which was probably their purpose. While the women gossiped, the children played in the street—duck-on-the-rock, prisoner's base, hopscotch with intricate variations—city games confined by space and rules, but exciting and played with every ounce of energy.

Into the fringe of this transplanted European world stepped the completely naïve one from Fitchburg. The two professions open in those days to untrained young ladies were teaching and social work, of all professions the two that most need a vocation. Though I had a vocation for neither, I was very early embarked on a combination of both. In a Jewish orphan asylum that saved the lives of hundreds of children from the most destitute of the Jewish immigrant families, I learned more in a year than in all my life before, and possibly more than I have ever learned in so short a time since.

The Triangle fire, which occurred before I came to New York, and the East Side ghetto may seem far-fetched for this personal record of events, but they had a bearing. They constituted a background which one could not escape. The fire had revolutionized social thinking. It affected insurance laws, building laws, labor laws. It startled the country's prosperous complacency. It aroused women to action from all walks of life—Ida Tarbell, Mary Simkovich, Mrs. O. H. P. Belmont, Henrietta Szold, Lillian Wald, Anne Morgan. Frances Perkins headed a Factory Investigating Commission after the Triangle disaster . . .

And the Lower East Side, though thirty miles from the green haven where I eventually landed, was always with us in the names and faces and eyes and memories of the institution children. Two of the little girls that I knew well had each lost an older sister in the fire. Many of the children had doubtless witnessed a pogrom. The father and mother of one of the boys had been killed before his eyes, in a village near Odessa . . .

IV

THE AVANT-GARDE OF 1913: *GEORGE'S LITTLE HOUSE*

It was out in Westchester County on the outskirts of the town of Pleasantville that the Hebrew Sheltering Guardian Society took care of these children of the desperately poor. With wisdom and tact, backed by sound organization, it probably saved the lives of many, and did wonders to promote their happiness.

The typical old-time orphan asylum, which this institution had originally been, was transformed in 1912. From a regimental life in an overcrowded single building at 150th Street and Broadway in Manhattan, it had moved into a group of pretty cottages surrounded by squares of greenery. The children, six hundred strong, led by a brass band, marched down from 150th Street to the 125th Street station on June 1, 1912. With a flare of triumphal drums they left

the pavements and their past, and in an hour found themselves in heaven. It was summer. The countryside opened
its arms to them, fragrant and fertile. And twenty cottages,
spotless in their newness, became their homes.

Each cottage had thirty children from six years of age
up to fourteen or fifteen. All the housework was done by
the children themselves under the eye of a trained Cottage
Mother. There was a brainy cousin of Justice Brandeis
among the Cottage Mothers, and a Mielziner of the scenic
design family, and a sister of a famous portrait painter. But
I never heard of temperaments getting out of hand. Perhaps
because of the novelty, or because it was fundamentally
sound, the system worked smoothly. I don't recall a serious
domestic problem the whole year I was there. An air of serenity permeated the entire children's village.

Both boys and girls cooked the kosher meals, and
washed and swept and polished the still shiny houses. Big
Brothers and Big Sisters (official titles) looked after Little
Brothers and Little Sisters. They saw that they were tucked
in at night, and that they made their beds in the morning,
with night clothes and towels neatly folded at the foot of
each child's bed—a far, far cry from Rivington Street
where the whole family slept and ate and worked in a single room.

Also in each Pleasantville cottage lived one or two
members of the school faculty with no prescribed duty toward the household, which made the relationship between
teachers and children much more natural and spontaneous
than is usual in this combination. We played evening games
together, took long country walks, sang around the piano,
talked books (*Sentimental Tommy, Tommy and Grizel,
Huck Finn*). It was good companionship—those bright-
eyed eager children and the young teachers not so much
older than the oldest of the children and some of them quite

as unsophisticated. A few of the older boys went back and forth daily to City College in New York.

Most of the children were actual orphans, some of them half-orphans, and a few the children of parents too ill or too desperately poor to keep them at home. On visiting day one saw what remnants of family they had. Perhaps a mother with a shawl over her *sheitl*, or a pale tubercular father, or an older sister already working in a factory or doing sweatshop work with a dozen others in a tenement. The meetings with relatives were apt to be awkward. Like the more fortunate children in boarding schools and summer camps, these boys and girls had already made a new life in their day-by-day contacts, which left them nothing to say to the old folks with their old ways.

The head of the institution—Dr. B., as he was always called (Dr. Ludwig Bernstein)—was way ahead of his time. He saw to it that the children under his care were warmly and intelligently loved. Their friendship with older people and the equable arrangement of work and responsibility among the boys and girls themselves did wonders in building up self-confidence, proof of which lies in the mark they made once they got out into the world. Offhand and without looking up any records, I recall half a dozen outstanding career figures that date from my time. The boy from Odessa, for instance, became a certified public accountant before he was twenty-one, and very early had a prosperous accounting business of his own. Another bright boy became the pioneer manufacturer of radio and television equipment, was first to make radio kits and sets for the home, first to equip an aircraft with short-wave apparatus for transmission and reception of messages. One of the girls became a fashion designer whose name used to be well known in the pages of *Vogue*. One boy (specializing in United States history at the beginning of the 19th century, and an authority on Aaron Burr) became a historical novelist. Another is a nationally admired bibliophile who has probably done more than any single person in this country to keep alive scarce and desirable books for library use.

The children had their own republic with officers and meetings, and fifty years later the practice still prevails to elect officers and hold meetings. In the old days of the barracks institution the boys called the girls "Crows" and the girls called them "Ravens." Now the "Crows and Ravens," a strong-timbered organization, has regular nostalgic get-togethers, and does what it can for children who a generation earlier wouldn't seem to have had a chance. In 1962 they celebrated their Golden Anniversary.

Nowadays the problems have changed. There is still a cottage colony, but it reflects the neurotic cast of the times. Instead of rescuing the povery-stricken from disease and filth in the slums, the institution and its willing alumni are now confronted with maladjusted and "disturbed" children. These are the ones who now live in Pleasantville, where the saplings have grown to be large shade trees.

In New York the children had gone to public school. In Pleasantville they had a school of their own. Whether by chance or because of personal preference, Dr. Bernstein assembled a faculty nearly all of whom were non-Jewish. Perhaps he did it to give his immigrant children as broad a view as possible of America. If so, he didn't altogether succeed, because it was not a typical America to which he introduced them through his hand-picked faculty. But he could not have assembled one with a truer sense of values. By whatever odd fluke of circumstances, this institution, which harbored the most destitute in the land, became a gathering place, for a short period, of a small group of intellectuals that was destined to send forth some conspicuously brilliant shafts of light.

It was the exact hour and the right soil for the germination of ideals. The college graduate of 1912 was more eager than his counterpart of today. One cannot be sure, because today's boys and girls, although highly articulate, keep their lips sealed about themselves. In those days they were less inhibited, more intrinsically sure of themselves, I'd say. There had not been a world war, two world wars, three wars. Cynicism was not tarnishing youth's bright hopes for humanity. The exceptional college graduate of that day would choose a position teaching Jewish orphans before he would try, let us say, to get into a publishing firm or a science lab.

To get the full flavor of that particular group of young people who found themselves together on the campus of the H.S.G.S. you must take out one box from inside another box, and out of it another box, and then another, like the Chinese toys. It was a small faculty and not of itself memorable. Harriet Works and Frankie Downes taught the little children. Harriet was a breezy New Englander, a girl of rare wit, daughter of an inventor and an original herself. Frankie was the sister of Olin Downes, future music critic of *The New York Times*, a tall graceful girl with a wealth of brown wavy hair tied at her neck and hanging way down her back. She was always casual. When she got married, we all rummaged through our belongings to find items she could use, or might like. We were getting forty dollars a month plus room and board, so we were casual too.

A boy from Dartmouth taught mathematics. A young minister, who left every Saturday night for Sunday at his own small parish, taught history. The manual training teacher was a naturalist and woodsman who took us—children and teachers—on long meandering country walks. Freda, exception to the non-Jewish theory, taught German. She was a person of wisdom, to whom we brought our problems, a friend in those days of the artists William Zorach and Jo Davidson, and intimate of a large Russian family fresh from Tolstoi's own region of Tula. (Tolstoi was a friend of the family's and I recall seeing a picture of him with his arm thrown affectionately around the shoulders of their grandfather.) Nearly every Sunday two of these three tall Russian sons wandered out onto the Pleasantville scene.

But there would have been no story without George Cronyn, who taught art.

George Cronyn had been to Harvard in the Great Days. Probably there are always Great Days at Harvard. But this was the day of "Copey" and Dean Briggs, the inspiration of three generations of writers; of William James, Royce and Münsterberg, Santayana and George Herbert Palmer. Socialism was making its first brilliant intellectual appeal through the Shavian Society, and liberal-minded Harvard boys were rushing over to Lawrence to picket for the underpaid mill workers in America's first big strike. It was the nurturing period for an impressive roster of undergraduates.

George was a genial soul and a good picker. He beckoned his friends to gather round wherever he might be, and the selection of ex-Harvard weekend guests who made a rendezvous of Pleasantville at his invitation have since made history.

I recall Walter Lippmann, in serious political discussion even then—with "G.M.," the only woman editorial writer, as I remember, on the New York *Sun.* The Boni brothers, Charles and Albert, also fresh from Harvard, used to come out on Thursday and stay until Tuesday. They were planning the American sequel to Lecky's *European Morals*, and were always jotting down notes. Egmont Arens, then a tubercular poet, now a heavy, husky industrial designer, was one of us, and Bobby Jones (Robert Edmond Jones), soon to become one of the foremost scenic designers and the only young man we knew to wear a beard. There was also Sam Eliot, grandson of the great Harvard president; Kenneth MacGowan, future movie producer; and Hiram Motherwell, erudite theatrical critic. Names already fading out of recognition, but formidable figures in the intellectual arena of our heyday.

George Cronyn had also gone to Columbia for a year, and, true to form, he drew out from New York's less sequestered halls the cream of that crop: Philip Moeller, fair-haired and blue-eyed, twirling a stick and speaking in epigrams, a dilettante then who later became the Theatre Guild's cleverest director, the catalytic agent for the highly successful Lunt-Fontanne team. Eddie Goodman, with the most elegant diction I have ever heard, on or off the stage, a director-to-be of the Washington Square Players, and backbone of the American School of Dramatic Arts, where he taught Spencer Tracy, Katharine Cornell, Fredric March and Florence Eldridge, Grace Kelly, Lauren Bacall, Kirk Douglas. English Lawrence Langner, renowned impresario of the future, a struggling young patent lawyer then, was a regular visitor. And Josephine Meyer, the heart of that group, playwright and actress, who frequently brought in her train a young writer named Harry Scherman.

George was a good provider. A little shack on the grounds of the institution was his for the asking. It was down the hill from the cottages and had once been the home of a Negro workman. It was about five minutes' walk through a small apple orchard, which has forever in my memory mingled the scent of apple blossoms with the heady fragrance of Aspiration, Inspiration and Ideals.

The soil behind the shack must have been fertile, for George made himself a garden of vegetables and flowers.

He built a fireplace and got a stove in some sort of working condition. Whenever we could we wandered down in the late afternoon and often in the evening. We sat around the open fire in winter, and under the apple trees in spring. We talked of Life, of Women's Suffrage, of Henry James and George Meredith and Thomas Hardy, Ibsen, Strindberg and Oscar Wilde. We tried to understand Bergson. Freud never entered the picture. And Sex was decently remote. We were in love with life, not with one another.

It was the thing to say in New York those days as Friday approached: "Going out to George's Little House?" Most of the guests came for a long all-day Sunday, bringing lunch with them which was laid out on one table for all. But there were others who found corners to sleep in for the weekend. The Boni boys and Eggie were stand-bys. The Russians supplied an accent, and Sasha, the taller of the two tall thin brothers, played the guitar. The boy from Dartmouth played a flute. Sometimes we danced, oftener we sang. "Hallelujah, I'm a Bum," "The Curse of an Aching Heart" ("You made me what I am today, I hope you're satisfied"). Someone was always ready to recite a Kipling Barrack Room Ballad. And we weren't above singing "My Melancholy Baby" or "Waiting for the Robert E. Lee" or "Mobile Bay."

But mostly it was serious talk. Or the light ball of wit tossed from Phil to Eggie to Ed to George. George did the cooking, if any, the girls present washed the dishes; and occasionally one of the older boys who went to City College joined us. It was all regulation and accepted by those in command. But George's Little House remained the gathering place of only a given few from the institution.

Those of us who knew it, and still sometimes speak of it, always do so with a rush of gratitude and warmth in our hearts. A kind of gentleness creeps into the voice when any of the old crowd speaks of that lovely time and place. One looks back on it as a Watteau scene on the hillside, the al fresco grouping, the long summer dresses that we wore, the merriment, the music.

But that was only one aspect. We who were living there were involved in a deep spiritual experience. Our hearts went out to those eager children transplanted from distant lands. We came to know them well and made friendships among them that hold to this day. It was a relationship that opened our minds to people and ideas undreamed of. It gave us a glimpse of the Old World and the infinite variety of the Jewish temperament. It was the door to New York.

V

BOHEMIA

New York's Bohemia before World War I was a spiritual haven. I doubt if ever in America there has been a spot where art and living, intertwined for a short time, brought forth such earnestness or such good companionship. It was a tiny island in the big city and its span of idyllic life was short—1912 to 1915. By 1916 it was already becoming self-conscious, and from then on through the years it has changed into the Village as we know it today—commercialized, somewhat cheapened, often unsavory. But to those of us who lived there in that halcyon day it is the essence of our youthful dreams.

We were young and free, and our values were singularly true. Life in Bohemia was serious, and its ethical standards were probably higher than in most of the parts from which we had come. The uptown rich of that day tended toward Edwardian tinsel. They were frivolous, and far more than now inclined to display. The less prosperous, the provincials, were still narrowly Victorian, probably in no place more so than in New England Fitchburg. In Bohemia there was no set code of conduct, but at the same time very few stood in judgment. People were thinking and acting for themselves. It was our Age of Reason.

I came to live there because New York was a lure, and I had the offer of a job. Bohemia was a close cousin of George's Little House. "There's a corner of New York, near Washington Square," Freda told me one day under an apple tree. "Some artists are living there . . ." Freda was a person of few words, and she never spoke unless she had something to say. It was the first I had ever heard of the region—this small segment that had been coming into its own over a period of several years. It was not yet commonly called by its historical name of Greenwich Village. It was not deliberately "Left Bank." The artists and writers and others with congenial temperaments who lived there did so because lodgings were cheap and the muddle of little streets with rows of low brick houses was pleasing. They found space in old houses, often in picturesque back alleys. They hadn't the money for renovations, and even if they had had, their sense of the fitting would have restrained them. From the edges of the Square and MacDougal Alley these eager pioneers spread gradually to the west into what had been the solidly Irish old Ward 9—to Charles and Grove and Perry and Bank streets; and south along Bleecker, Bedford and Carmine, and Minetta Lane, where Italians, mostly from the north of Italy, had shortly preceded them. Seventh Avenue ended in those days at Eleventh Street.

Few Bohemians could afford to live on the Square itself. The large pink-brick Georgian houses on the north side still bore the brass doorplates of Van Rensselaer, Stewart, Lydig, Rhinelander. This was still Henry James's New York. The beautiful Arch, designed by Stanford White not too many years before (1895), gave it a look of Paris. The trees and the grass were green, the paths were precise. On the south side of the Square the Judson Memorial had long since attracted a few famous painters to its tower rooms. George Innes had once been a tenant. And north of the Square at a later day John Sargent had had a studio on Tenth Street.

For the newcomers in my time, "studio" was a term not commonly used, perhaps because of its prosperous professional connotation. Most of the artists lived and worked in one room. Climbing two or three flights of stairs didn't matter, but a view of roof tops did, a slanting back yard with a tree. A south window was heaven—for warmth—or a north one for clear light. One thing all these habitations had in common was inconvenience. Roofs leaked. Windows rattled. Rooms were cold and draughty. A lucky few had fireplaces, but oftener a small wood stove or a kerosene burner. Many of the houses had no bathroom and it was not an uncommon sight to see a man or woman, towel on arm, making for the house of one of the old-timers—someone in the money—to borrow a bath before evening.

These free spirits were easy to please. They had escaped from gridiron streets uptown, or from families, or from conventionality. They were free but not loose. Alcohol and sex had not yet taken over. Down there in the shadow of the Arch almost everyone worked hard and lived austerely. Evenings only were for play. Few drank anything stronger than the bitter Chianti they bought from the neighboring Italians. (I for one never had a cocktail until after I was married.) Of course there were the notable exceptions, like Eugene O'Neill. But he was only a casual visitor, not a real resident. Serious drinking was still in the future.

It was the day of woman's emancipation. Free love, woman's suffrage, Lucy Stone ideals, all are melded in memory with the vision of strong purposeful women— magnificent women some of them, like Inez Milholland, tall handsome Vassar girl, leading a suffrage parade; and Crystal Eastman, beautiful Junoesque law student fighting for the downtrodden; Henrietta Rodman, high school teacher, a plain woman, but with powerful personality and influence, who after school hours donned sacklike garments as a protest against the still prevalent whalebones and corsets, and preached against the hypocrisy of the double standard and legal marital ties.

Free love was not illicit self-indulgence, as the conventional world of that day chose to regard it. It was a serious ethical undertaking. Unmarried couples in this starry-eyed Bohemia lived together openly and proudly, two names on the mailbox, two separate individualities facing the world. Looking back, it seems as if they outnumbered the married couples two to one. But one couldn't always tell. Married or unmarried, the women, true Lucy Stoners, kept their own names. And I remember no sly innuendoes or whispers. These were earnest women who refused to be bound by law to the man they loved, and the circle in which they lived respected their independence. The men for the most part were artists and writers, young, idealistic, many of them talented, who had not yet got a hearing. The women were the wage-earners and supported them through these two or three vital struggling years—school teachers, professional writers, more than one modestly paid social worker, a successful commercial photographer. What happened to the men in later years the world knows. Several have become famous. But the names of the women have been forgotten. Their faces I remember only dimly, but their vivid personalities, clearly. Their subsequent histories would make a fascinating postscript to the social customs of a very special period in our culture. Doubtless in due time they married, and are now happy grandmothers writing their memoirs.

This little world so filled with verve and spirit might have been on another planet. Where all the people came from I didn't know until much later, nor did I care. As to what the future might hold for them or for myself, I never gave it a thought. Nor to what lay behind me in New England. The present absorbed us all.

No one ever sees farther then the circumference of a small circle, and I have tried to recall only what I actually saw in one corner of New York in that refreshing, short interlude.

The gathering place was Polly's, an eating place in the basement of 135 MacDougal Street. There weren't many restaurants in the region at that time, and those few were scattered. Gonfarone's Italian table d'hôte at Eighth Street and MacDougal Alley was too expensive for most of us. The Brevoort and the Lafayette were way beyond us. But how we cherished them! I can think of no hostelries before or since—or in any country—of such distinct personality, so completely congenial and so hospitable. On occasion we visited them late in the evening. That would be for a long drawn-out cup of coffee, or a bottle of wine which had to do for a tableful. I remember specifically sitting in the Brevoort café one summer evening at the table with Lucy Huffaker, a young journalist with prematurely white hair, who was smoking a cigarette in a long holder. "Lady smoking" presented a spectacle so rare that a crowd of urchins gathered outside in the shadows to stare.

But the heart of Bohemia pulsed evenly and regularly at Polly's. You went down two steps into a low-ceilinged room, and there were four wooden trestle tables with long benches always well filled. Polly, a quite young woman, tall and thin, with hair severely pulled back, took care of the cooking; and Hippolyte Havel, an explosive little man with a big mustache, waited on table. Hippolyte had come from Hungary and Europe in general, where he had served time in several prisons as an anarchist. Polly—though it was all but impossible to believe it in the light of her looks and her demeanor—had come to New York from Evanston, Illinois, because she too was an anarchist. Among the artists who frequented her restaurant were Andrew Dasberg, tall rangy Viking with a limp; Marsden Hartley, pale and mysterious-looking; the two robust Zorachs, conventionally married and living with their baby upstairs over a store on Tenth Street beside the Jefferson Market Court; Maurice Becker, with round beaming face, always there—as were his pictures, hanging on Polly's walls; cartoonists Art Young and Boardman Robinson.

There were more writers than artists, I think. Max Eastman, teaching at Columbia, was already working on *The Enjoyment of Poetry* and shortly to be the editor of *The Masses* magazine. Floyd Dell, usually with a red muffler around his neck, seemed to suffer from a perpetual cold. He had come from Iowa by way of Chicago, and was writing a novel. Mary Heaton Vorse, already successful as a short-story writer, was one of the few who owned and lived in a whole house; Inez Haynes Gillmore was writing suffrage novels; Upton Sinclair, only an occasional guest, had *The Jungle* already behind him. Among the poets were Orrick Johns, a short lame man said to have stepped out of the world of wealth and convention; Harry Kemp, not yet known as the Tramp Poet, always without a hat in the day when every man wore one; Alfred Kreymborg; Gilbert Seldes, poet before he became a journalist.

A tall white-haired figure with cape flung over his shoulders, always at Polly's, was George Cram Cook, known to all as Jig, and well loved. From Davenport, Iowa, Jig was soon to be the inspiration of the Provincetown Players and the impresario who would introduce Eugene O'Neill to the world. He later became an ardent Hellenist, spent his last years in Greece and was buried in Delphi. The one who made all this possible was Susan Glaspell, his small, even-tempered wife, who wrote industriously and successfully while Jig dreamed, took care of him, and in the end immortalized him in her beautiful book *The Road to the Temple*.

Theater was in the air. There was Helen Westley, a dark, rather sinister-looking woman, later to star with the Washington Square Players, but in those days silent in a corner bent over a book; and Ralph Roeder, a pale young actor who later wrote *Man of the Renaissance*, and at that time looked himself like an early Florentine portrait. Also Lawrence Langner, of George's Little House, outgoing and friendly to all.

The Boni boys were always there, inseparable, this year moving on from *A History of Morals* to a bookstore, then publishing, and theater planning. Theirs was the original Washington Square Bookshop, located at that time over Polly's and still operating in the 1960's, but under another roof and another owner. It was in their bookshop over Polly's that the idea for the Washington Square Players was born—the band of players who in time became the nucleus of the Theatre Guild.

Horace Traubel, short stocky little man with lined face and shock of white hair, linked our world with Walt Whitman's. Many an evening I remember sitting around a table listening to Traubel reminiscing about his old friend Walt.

Upstairs over the restaurant was the Liberal Club. Whether Polly's was responsible for the spirit of the Lib-

eral Club or the Liberal Club for Polly's, it would be hard
to say. They were one. You ate downstairs night after night,
and sat there indefinitely; or you wandered upstairs and listened indefinitely to animated discussions. Or danced to a
tinny piano. It was a far cry from the dissipations of Greenwich Village in the twenties. It was even farther from the
languors and general sliminess of its present-day beatniks.
No arty shops, no quaint restaurants, no lurid night clubs.

In 1913 three girls lived on the top floor of No. 28
Grove Street, a solid brick house built in the late 1820's
when New Yorkers who had moved up into the village of
Greenwich to escape the plague were beginning to settle in
and build themselves town houses. In terms of the original
family, the top floor would have been the servants' quarters.
But just before our day it had been made over for rental
purposes to comprise a living room, a dining room, bedroom and kitchen. And we added to its capacities by making it into two bed-living rooms on the north side, a sub-
leased apartment on the south, and a shared kitchen. (One
bathroom served the house. It was two flights down, and
used by the landlord and his family who lived on the first
floor, all the tenants on our floor, and those on the floor between.)

All four rooms of our apartment opened onto a narrow
hallway at the top of the stairs, into which were piled the
trunks of the three girls and the tenant couple. Suitcases,
like automobiles, had not yet come into full recognition.
Since closet and drawer space was at a premium on the top
floor, many of our belongings had to remain in the trunks,
which were constantly being shifted, lifted or pushed aside.
The inconvenience from this distance seems all but insurmountable. But we never gave it a thought. We were al-

ways in a hurry and sharp corners were everywhere. Legs were forever black-and-blue from bumps.

We had rented the best room of our apartment to a close friend of Jack Reed's, and that eager and very winning young man was racing up and down the two flights many times a week.

Marsden Hartley, our next-door neighbor, had a painting in the much heralded Armory Show, to which we all went—we Bohemians—open-minded and undismayed. It was America's introduction to Picasso and Matisse and the famous "Nude Descending a Staircase" of Duchamp, all of which we took in our stride. The names of Gertrude Stein and Leo Stein and of John Quinn were already familiar to us. Uptown New York went to the Armory Show for a laugh. But we of Grove Street, though we might not have been able to define modern art or differentiate among its various trends, felt honestly that we were present at an epoch-making occasion.

Uptown New York scarcely knew of the existence of the Liberal Club. But it was quite aware of another Bohemian center. At Ninth Street and Fifth Avenue, in the white-painted second-floor apartment of an old brownstone, lived Mabel Dodge, a young matron of money from Buffalo, New York, by way of Florence, Italy, who had begun to surround herself with intellectual luminaries. Mabel Dodge's salon was Bohemia's gathering place, not of the poor artists but of the more or less recognized intelligentsia. Among her regulars were Carl Van Vechten, music critic of the *Times* and champion of the inarticulate Negro; again Walter Lippmann, just returned from Schenectady where he had briefly been secretary to the socialist mayor, George Lunn, and already writing his *Preface to Politics;* Lincoln Steffens, chief of the muckrakers; Ernest Poole, who had not yet written *The Harbor;* Hutchins Hapgood of the *Globe*—mighty intellects perhaps but, for the carefree young, without charm.

Mabel Dodge's evenings made news. She promoted discussion from all fronts except the conservative. One night she would invite the anarchists Emma Goldman and her friend Alexander Berkman, lately released from prison in California where he had been serving time for the shooting of Henry Clay Frick. Another evening would be devoted to the I.W.W.'s represented by "Big Bill" Haywood, the one-eyed giant, and Carlo Tresca, both in wide black hats, and Elizabeth Gurley Flynn, the young revolutionary then in her thirties, with bright blue eyes and a cloud of black Irish hair, earnest and self-abnegating.

We knew these characters and also about these evenings. We knew what they discussed. But few of those who patronized the Liberal Club participated. The headliners of the Dodge group, already beginning to be known because of their writings or their radical activities, seemed older. Any gap in years at that age seems enormous, and the prominence of their names removed these particular figures still further.

The only ones who really "belonged" at Mabel Dodge's were the socialists. The anarchists were more at home in their hall on Lenox Avenue—before the days of black Harlem. Here they held their Saturday night meetings, two or three of which I attended. They were surprisingly gentle folk. I came to know Emma Goldman's nephew well, who later became a figure in the literary world as editor Saxe Commins, and her beautiful niece Stella, married to actor Teddy Ballantine. Emma Goldman was a plain, red-haired woman, and Berkman, for all his sinister reputation, was mild and quiet-spoken. Of all the political groups which I have ever come up against I felt easiest with these—the anarchists.

The I.W.W.'s, "the Wobblies," were far and away

the most stimulating radicals of that day—or of any day perhaps up to the Spanish Civil War. The anarchists on the whole were theorists, but the Wobblies were right out there fighting. It was the time of the big Paterson silk strike—to New York what the Lawrence strike had been to industrial Massachusetts. On and off for twelve years the Paterson workers had been striking for higher wages and a shorter workday. But the newspapers gave them no space and the public was kept in ignorance—until Mabel Dodge's little coterie, for once acting instead of talking, took matters into their own hands.

"Big Bill" Haywood was their Savonarola. One evening, fresh from Paterson, he told the Serious Thinkers at Mabel Dodge's about the strike that had now been going on for two months. More than twenty thousand men and women were out. They were hungry and nearly penniless, and there were daily arrests. Yet the picket line stood firm. That very day he had come from the funeral of Valentine Modestino, a picketer who was shot and killed by the police. Fifteen thousand mourning workers had followed Modestino's body to the grave, and then gone back to the picket line. Their courage was indomitable. Yet no one would give them a hearing.

Jack Reed was in the group of listeners. Reed was then living at 42 Washington Square South with two or three of his Harvard cronies. He was Bohemia's Golden Boy—poet, successful magazine writer, gay companion, eager, impetuous, equally at ease with big shots like Irwin Cobb or James Montgomery Flagg and his penniless Washington Square companions. Lincoln Steffens was his mentor; Mabel Dodge only later became his love, and then not for long.

That evening when he heard Bill Haywood describing the heroism of the Paterson workers was perhaps the turn-

ing point in his career. The next day Reed himself went out
to Paterson. The strikers were denied the right of assembly,
so he talked to them on the porches of their homes, and for
this he was arrested. When the police asked him what his
work was, he answered, "Poet." He was sentenced to
twenty days in jail and served four, thus making headlines
in the New York papers, which was the best thing to date
that had happened to the strikers. As Harvard cheer leader
he knew the value of song for keeping up courage, and he
taught the strikers to sing.

April 19 was the day Modestino had been buried. And
on June 7, Reed staged the famous pageant in Madison
Square Garden which commemorated the martyr's death,
and placed the helplessness of the Paterson workers
squarely before the public. The pageant was conceived by
Reed, ably assisted by Ernest Poole; scenically designed by
Bobby Jones, then one of the indigent Harvard companions
(actually it was the first professional stage work of Robert
Edmond Jones); and paid for by Mabel Dodge and her
friends.

No one who was in Madison Square on the night of
June 7 will ever forget the exhilaration of that mass meeting. Madison Square Garden was then on the northeast
corner of the square, and that night the square was a sea
of people. As soon as it was dark a huge "I.W.W." shone
forth in electric lights high on the tower—the tower where
Stanford White had been shot in a faraway day. It had
been wired surreptitiously and the insignia in all its brilliance burst upon the unaware onlookers like a bomb.

Inside on the platform Jones had built a panorama of
the Paterson mills. They were approached by a long runway through the audience over which plodded a thousand
workers brought over from Paterson for the occasion.
There were several episodes: the mill whistle sounded, the

workers filed in, the looms banged, and gradually behind the noise of the looms could be heard the rising strains of the "Marseillaise." The climax was the funeral with a bier on which the workers dropped twigs of evergreen. Haywood and Elizabeth Flynn gave short, stirring orations. Then the audience joined with the strikers and marched solemnly out out of the hall, singing.

Bohemia was on the side of the I.W.W.'s to a man. It was a young movement. It embodied and dramatized newly roused sentiments against bad labor conditions. Like the Lawrence strike which had had ardent Harvard help, and the Triangle fire so close to the hearts of New Yorkers, the Paterson strike and the pageant made an unforgettable impression on the serious-minded.

Ida Tarbell, Lincoln Steffens, Upton Sinclair and all the other muckrakers had already done a job of uncovering the evils of big business; Danish Jacob Riis had written up the personal miseries of the Lower East Side in *How the Other Half Lives*. As the first news photographer he had shown it so graphically that Theodore Roosevelt, then governor, came down from Albany and spent a whole day with Riis, inspecting the tenements to find out where sweatshops were operating and how the Factory Law was working. Settlement houses were attracting girls and boys from college: Hull House in Chicago, West End House in Boston, the Henry Street Settlement in New York. Young businessmen were taking on boys' clubs.

But the I.W.W. was different. It was "socialism in working clothes," as Haywood said. No one who saw the Paterson strike pageant was likely ever again to think of the working class as an indefinable mass. It was the tragedies of individuals that were enacted before our eyes. It was a glimpse into another world, only a glimpse, it is true, but an important one for many. It opened our minds to the

West Virginia miners spurred on by Mother Jones, the only American woman that thousands of foreign workers had ever spoken to; to the Ludlow coal miners' strike that same year in Colorado, where the militia fired on the tent colony of women and children and killed twelve . . .

"Pass the eight-hour day!" was the slogan. It's hard at this late date to realize how new the idea of injustice was, and how important the labor troubles of the early twentieth century loomed. "Proletariat" was not yet a term. Nor was "Red." After all, it was fifty years ago.

The Bohemia of 1913 was a small stage. One could see around it. The faces of many of its inhabitants were etched in my memory for all time. I was aware of its deep seriousness and its dignity of purpose. And I was never to lose the excitement of those first dramatic encounters in New York.

But I was more an onlooker than a true Bohemian. I was on the fringe.

VI

BROADWAY

New York was whirling itself into the great metropolis it was later to become, rich and gay and pleasure-loving. It's true, the artists and writers and dedicated intellectuals pursuing their idealistic careers in the corner near Washington Square paid it scant attention. But I was a hybrid, and as such had my own mild little fling both uptown and down.

That year, my first in New York, and the last before the Great War, the theater was paradise—a dream world that needed but the raising of the curtain night after night to come to life. I found it irresistible. But at twenty I was already an old hand.

Theater-going for me had started long before I got to New York. It began when I was a child, on trips to Boston with my mother, and my aunt, and my grandmother.

It began before 1910 and has run uninterruptedly from then to now. Even last night! The lights of the marquee have never failed to lure me.

In those days long ago, plays were a year late getting to Boston instead of opening there, as often happens now. Shows were red hot in New York, warmed up in Boston. But to us at the Hollis, or the Colonial, or the Tremont, or the Park, the productions were pristine in their freshness.

I've always thought I saw the original Floradora Sextet, but now I'm not sure. The girls that I saw I remember distinctly: compact beauties wearing lavender gowns and long black gloves, nodding the black plumes that drooped over their hat brims, and twirling lavender parasols. But I've learned since that there were sixty-seven replacements in the first year, so fast did these fascinating girls marry off, or otherwise better themselves financially. I know that I missed Nan Paterson (accused of murder) and Evelyn Nesbit (the cause of murder) and Marie Wilson (who became a millionaire overnight on stock-market tips from a big-time admirer).

Donald Brian and Ethel Jackson played Boston in the original *Merry Widow* and I was there. Also at *The Red Mill* with Fred Stone and Dave Montgomery, which still holds its own with the best in musical shows—with *Show Boat*, *My Fair Lady*, and everything else that Herbert himself wrote.

"Six months after I'm dead," Victor Herbert once said, and apparently believed, "no one will remember my name." In Saratoga Springs in the 1930's, when the Grand Union Hotel was still standing in all its magnificence of enormous rooms, tall pillars and porchful of rocking chairs, and an army of waiters carrying trays on their heads, the manager told us that Victor Herbert had conducted his orchestra in the hotel garden for many seasons, and that he sometimes passed the baton to a little boy, son of the manager at that time, who was always underfoot. The little boy was Monty Woolley (*The Man Who Came to Dinner*), and Saratoga was Herbert's stamping ground because besides being a conductor and composer he was also an enthusiastic gambler.

Back in the Boston days I saw *The Three Twins* with Bessie McCoy, petite wife of Richard Harding Davis. Dressed in black satin pajamas with white ruff, shaking her wild blond hair, she threw herself into angles singing "Yama-Yama Man."

I sobbed over David Warfield in *The Music Master;* was terrified—horrified—and still am in retrospect—over *A Fool There Was:* "A rag, a bone, and a hank of hair . . ." and the human disintegration of the man who had let them destroy him. It was Robert Hilliard who stumbled down the stairs right stage and fell on his face before the pale black-haired vampire who turned on her high heel and walked out on him.

There was Forbes-Robertson in *The Light That Failed* —the room getting darker and darker as the truth of his blindness came over him. And E. H. Sothern as Lord Dundreary in *Our American Cousin.* They say that when Sothern's father played the part before him, he once stubbed his toe by mistake on his first entrance. This so wowed the house that from then on to the next generation, Lord Dundreary stumbled on his first appearance and thus created one of the great comedy characters in stage history.

A Gentleman from Mississippi was played by big Tom Wise (later Falstaff in *The Merry Wives*) and a handsome young juvenile whose name one would never have remembered, had it not happened to be Douglas Fairbanks.

Boston and I saw Maude Adams in *The Little Minis-*

ter, *Quality Street* and *What Every Woman Knows*. Between them, Barrie and Maude Adams gave every girl confidence, however young she might be, because the women in their plays were so wise and the men so callow. With today's slant toward the neurotic and the unrestrained in show people it is hard to believe how romantic we of that day found the rather prim and highly respectable Maude Adams.

Peter Pan, the biggest hit of the Barrie-Maude Adams combine, I somehow missed in its first cast. I know that it opened November 6, 1905, at the Empire Theater in New York, and that in some incarnation it is probably still playing.

(Incidentally, the Empire far outlasted the other old turn-of-the-century New York theaters, dripping sentiment and nostalgia from its red brocaded walls and heavy velvet carpets, portraits of Henry Irving, Mansfield, Maude Adams and Ethel Barrymore looking complacently down from the lobby walls upon new theater audiences that scarcely knew their names. I remember vividly two later opening nights at the Empire. In 1918 an eighteen-year-old girl played Barrie's *Dear Brutus*. She was unknown to most of that first-night audience, a fair-haired, blue-eyed girl who looked for all the world like a young Maude Adams, and who played her part with the same breathless eagerness. The sentimental audience buzzed excitedly. Could it be that unbeknownst to all Maude Adams was secretly married and that Helen Hayes was her daughter? Of course the papers put us straight the next day—but there was a moment!

Another famous first night at the Empire was in November, 1939. It was the opening of Clarence Day's *Life With Father*. For that play of old New York, the Empire was the perfect setting, and to underline the atmosphere, when the play was over the audience found a line of horse-drawn carriages pulled up at the theater entrance, corralled by the management from their regular stand at the Plaza and Central Park.

In the spirit of *Father*'s 1890's, four of us stepped into one of the carriages and drove over to Fifth Avenue and up to the Plaza. It was a gala occasion. The other man in the carriage was Ben Huebsch, one of the most perspicacious publishers in the book world, but not so perspicacious that night about the theater. "A nice little period piece," he said, "but it won't last two weeks."

He had loved it; we all had loved it; the audience was bowled over. But it was a first night and you never can tell, said Ben. He made a bet with my husband that if *Life With Father* lasted three months, he would treat him to the best seats for any show in town. As everyone knows, it was still playing in February, 1947.)

But to get on with 1913—out of Boston now, and down in New York. In 1913 there were 162 shows on Broadway (as against 54 in 1962-63), and of the 162 I saw 52.

Theater in those days was strictly top balcony—steep climbs up uncarpeted old-board stairs; walls marked up with other climbers' symbols and fancies; excitement, anticipation, and final breathless arrival. Then the steeper descent to one's seat—the first two rows fifty cents, the others thirty-five. In all but the front row one had to sit sideways for knee-space, feet in the fur neckpiece of the lady immediately below, or the shiny Arrow collar of her escort. All around was laughter, talk and greenroom gossip. No one in orchestra seats could possibly know the fun that went on up there, or the expert theater knowledge that the habitués brought with them and shared.

Can it be the same now, I often wonder. I could find out easily enough—I often walk past the second-balcony entrances of the few old theaters that still have them, and I see those stairs. But I don't climb them. I only look. And it's not only I. These days the lowest-priced seats are the last in the house to sell, I hear. People are getting soft. Or rich.

But what a season it was!

Otis Skinner in rags sat beside a pool of real water and begged, in *Kismet*. A girl in diaphanous garment ran gracefully down a runway over the heads of the audience in *Sumurun* (import from Germany and Reinhardt). George Arliss was the one and only *Disraeli*. For a whole generation in America, no one could possibly visualize Beaconsfield with any other face, or with anything but the consummate dignity of that final gesture when he gave his right hand to Lady Beaconsfield and, preceded by dukes and duchesses, moved slowly forward to meet his Queen.

Laurette Taylor played *Peg o' My Heart*. Doris Keane broke our hearts in *Romance*, which took place in the beloved Brevoort. It was by Edward Sheldon, not long out of Harvard, and before the terrible years of his crippling arthritis.

The Irish Players came over with Sara Allgood and Cathleen Nesbitt, dear friends of all of us who listened in on the Washington Square Players as they planned and schemed at Polly's. They gave the best of Lady Gregory, Yeats, St. John Irwin and Lennox Robinson. *Damaged Goods*, by Eugène Brieux, was so controversial (venereal disease) that for a time it was legally open only to members of the medical profession, but somehow I managed to see it. *The Affairs of Anatol* was played by the youngest and least known of the Barrymores, John.

. . .

Fortunately for my theater education, my paid job of social work during this time was "in the field." I was mistress of my time, provided I brought in the information I was sent out to get. This enabled me to catch the Monday afternoon show at the Palace, which, though only recently opened, was already the Mount Everest for all vaudevillians. Every Monday at one o'clock the Palace put on its new bill, and a handful of fans were there, ready to sit in judgment. They were mostly men, but among them, especially if it was a rainy Monday, was the social worker with bag of notes under her arm. (This was theater-going outside the count of fifty-two.) I always went alone. And so, apparently, did all the others. It was a very special, very individualistic audience.

Vaudeville in those days had all the ingredients of the best musicals of today without any of the pretense and bombast and Agnes de Mille-Jerome Robbins ballets. The acts were humor or skill or sentiment (songs). They had to be sharp, because there was little help from props. There were acrobats from France, dogs from the Bowery, soft-shoe tap competing with hard-shoe tap.

Chestnut-haired Nora Bayes with her heavy contralto and her equally heavy figure put over any song she sang with the same éclat that Ethel Merman gave hers a generation later. She sang "Shine On, Harvest Moon" with husband Jack Norworth. Also "Smarty" and "Take Me Out to the Ball Game," all of them written by Norworth. After Jack and Nora broke up, Nora continued to travel the boards, alone now except for short periods of succeeding husbands and a string of accompanists, one of whom was George Gershwin.

Among the Palace headliners were Elsie Janis before she became the "Sweetheart of the A.E.F."; the Dolly Sisters, Roziska and Yansci, Hungarian forerunners of the Gabor sisters, before they wore diamonds; Eddie Foy before there were Seven Little Foys. Harry Lauder swished his kilt, smirking and singing "A Wee Deeoch-an-Doris"; and Eva Tanguay flung herself around in a frenzy of "I Don't Care."

I saw Eva Tanguay the first time with the young minister who taught history at the Hebrew Sheltering Guardian. It was a Friday night. For professional reasons Saturdays were out for him. And before the show he took me to dinner. We had fried scallops and bacon, but Friday being my day for religious scruples, I gave him the bacon. All of which must have been out of bounds for a Baptist minister.

That year everybody was dancing. Vernon and Irene Castle, young, sprightly and good-looking, had taken over the country. They danced the Castle Walk, the Grizzly Bear, the Maxixe—as did we all. Irene wore chiffon, always chiffon, a cloud of pale blue-gray chiffon, the skirt twelve yards wide, the cuffs of pale gray fox. They danced the Turkey Trot: "Everybody's Doin' It" . . . "You Made Me Love You (I Didn't Want To Do It) . . ." One time by chance they fell into a new step which caught on immediately, both with them and the public. They called it the Fox Trot. There were *thés dansants*. People dancing everywhere.

All was not ballroom dancing. Isadora Duncan was undulating to the lilting measures of "The Blue Danube" played by a full symphony orchestra. In the exact center front of the stage, her bare feet slowly rising to the toes on each beat, her round knees in intoxicating rhythm, her Greek draperies slowly swaying, she tore her audience to pieces. Even Pavlova, The Swan, with her infinite grace and variety, didn't bring the moan of joy that the sensuous movements of Isadora roused. (Someone said that Isadora Duncan in her later years danced like a naked Cabot. And someone else said, the Cabots are never naked.)

The Diaghilev Ballet, which came over a little later—not that year, but still a long, long time ago—forever spoiled all other ballet for me, including the Russian. Curiously enough, I have met two dancers from the Diaghilev within the last few years. One was on the other side of the world in 1957. The Royal Hotel in Katmandu, Nepal, is run by Boris Lissanovitch, who danced in Paris under Prokofieff and Stravinsky and Monteux, and was in the opening of *The Three-Cornered Hat*, where Picasso, as scenic designer, got his first real recognition. Boris told us about it late into the night in his Nepalese garden. The second occasion was last year at a party in New York. There we met a tall, more than middle-aged Russian. When the talk turned to ballet I asked him if he'd ever read the autobiography of a Russian ballet dancer who had been a boy of fourteen at the time of the Revolution. I had read the book years ago and it just came back to me then out of the blue—one of the best personal accounts of that period that I had ever read. The name, I said, escaped me. The gentleman smiled and bowed. "It was I," said he. Some telepathic message had reached me. His name was Igor Schwezoff, and the book, *Borzoi*, had come out in 1931. After he left Russia he too danced in the Diaghilev troupe.

There was also that girl at the Winter Garden. Another of the good company of George's Little House was in love with a girl in the dancing chorus of the Al Jolson show at the Winter Garden. He adored her from afar and once took me there so that he could feast his eyes upon her. She *was* pretty, and she *could* dance. Her name was Marilyn Miller.

Restaurants have never since been so alluring.

Murray's Roman Garden, on West Forty-second Street, was a dream world of pink-shaded lights, mirrors, soft music and a revolving dance floor. In 1957 (again), my husband and I, in Hong Kong, met two English ladies, the Misses Aileen and Doris Woods, identical twins in their seventies. They were well known and respected in the Crown Colony. One worked in a bank, the other on Radio Hong Kong. When we met, they were coquettishly dressed in wine-red gowns with small blue-flower hats. The Woods girls had been a song-and-dance sister act, they told us, and forty-six years before they'd sung in Murray's, New York. When we met, half a century later, taking tea with them at the Peninsula Hotel in Kowloon, it was not hard to visualize the two pretty blondes of 1911. We didn't tell them that Murray's was later tenanted by the Flea Circus.

At Shanley's, Forty-third Street, where the Paramount now stands, you did not dance. The lights were bright and the patrons well fed. Of Shanley's I recall only steak and a vision of George M. Cohan, Mr. Popular, who was a regular patron.

Rector's, with its overtones of plush immorality, I never knew. Its heyday was unfortunately slightly before my own, but I knew its implications. In the final scene of *The Easiest Way* (which I *did* see), Frances Starr put on her feather boa, dabbed perfume on neck and arms, and said with cynical recklessness: "To Rector's!" as the curtain fell.

Reisenweber's was up on Eighth Avenue near Fifty-seventh Street in the region known as Hell's Kitchen. It was "sporty," and one felt that the girls present might well have come off the streets in the neighborhood.

Far and away the smartest French restaurant was Bustanoby's at Sixth Avenue and Fortieth Street, presided over by the cheery M. Bustanoby himself. On Saturday nights it was top of the town.

Except for Rector's, I knew a little of all these places,

but none well. Childs' was my milieu—any Childs', with
the familiar white-tiled bathroom-like walls and a girl flip-
ping pancakes in the window. But the Fourteenth Street
Childs' was the regular Village rendezvous.

Still oftener we went to Riggs. There was more than
one Riggs, but the one most favored in Grove Street days
was on Twentieth near Sixth Avenue. The trademark of
Riggs was a basket of sweet rolls on every table. As you sat
down, there they were, waiting for you, and before you got
your meal, every roll was eaten.

Companionship with the Russians from Tula opened
up a foreign country within New York. The actual Russian
restaurants burgeoned only after 1917, with the big exodus
of generals and princes and Romanoffs. Even then they did
not settle in in New York as they did in Paris. And it was
well into the twenties before the New York Russian restaurants took hold. But the Hungarians were already installed;
they were Old World—and to spare. On Second Avenue
there was Café Boulevard, and opposite it Café Monopole
where our Sasha played chess sometimes all day and way
into the night, his thin face gravely bent over the board.
Farther east was Little Hungary, already popular with uptowners; and still deeper in the Lower East Side were other,
smaller Hungarian eating places—the smaller, the more
foreign—all complete with chicken paprika, goulash, palat-
schinken, straight out of the Austrian Empire and far
removed from the beans and brown bread of Fitchburg,
Massachusetts. The entire transaction of the meal in these
little East Side spots was carried out by the waiter. Nothing
appeared on paper. There was no bill, the order was in his
head, the payment made directly into his old black wallet,
and change extracted from loose coins in his pockets. In
their shabby green-black suits and worn-down shoes, these

pale-faced wraiths from the Old Country might as well still have been back there, in Ljubljana or Budapest, for all they saw outside those steamy walls.

The persons and places and events of New York of that day were the texture of existence through which my own minute thread wove its faint pattern. In that world the Vernon Castles stood to my young eyes for grace and charm; the Isidor Strauses who went down together on the *Titanic* represented marital fidelity; the Lefty Louis-Lt. Becker-Herman Rosenthal case was Crime. I saw the Castles once, I never saw the Strauses, though I was later to wheel a baby-carriage into the little triangular park at Broadway and 105th Street that commemorates them. As for the Herman Rosenthal murder, I got only as close to it as the Metropole restaurant on West Forty-third Street where it took place. But even now when I walk through that block I remember the lurid details, just as I recall the horrors of the Triangle fire whenever I am on the east side of Washington Square. The records of these melodramatic events left far deeper impressions than comparable happenings of today, however tragic or evil the present may be.

The murder of Herman Rosenthal and the criminal world that it uncovered was an exposure of corruption in high office which was all but incomprehensible to a girl so recently come from the city of Patrolman Young. But it was also a topnotch crime story to which the papers did more than full justice, thus fostering a taste for murder mysteries, newspaper and otherwise, which in my case has not yet been satiated.

Beginning in 1912 the New York *World*, which was probably the best New York newspaper ever published, ran a series of articles on the tie-up between high police officials and the disreputable elements of the city, a relationship then at its peak. The *World* gave names and places, supplying the addresses of specific gambling houses and brothels that were paying for protection. For the underworld this was dynamite, and for the right-minded indignant public it was waving the banner of decency. To appease the respectable elements, Lt. Charles Becker, one of the chiefs of the strong-arm squad charged with the duty of suppressing gambling and vice, ordered a raid on the most notorious of the Broadway dives, the gambling house of Herman Rosenthal. The raid was carried out, Rosenthal's nephew was arrested on the premises, uniformed police were stationed at the house to prevent its reopening, and the public was momentarily appeased.

That was in April.

In early July, Herman Rosenthal made a public statement. He gave it to District Attorney Charles A. Whitman, and then to the New York *World*. In it he announced that he had been double-crossed by a prominent member of the police force, an officer who was himself a partner in the very business which he now saw fit to betray, and took a regular share of the profits. Rosenthal stated that the raid was a frame-up, that he himself had been warned it was coming, and so got out, and that his nephew was only a figurehead, innocent as a newborn lamb. He named Lt. Charles Becker.

Becker denied everything, and Rosenthal got warnings to beat it out of town before it was too late. But Rosenthal was now on the side of the angels. He not only stayed in town, he promised the D.A. that he would testify before the Grand Jury.

We are now up to July 15. The night after his promise to testify, Rosenthal was at the Metropole, an all-night hangout for actors, gamblers and politicians. It was 2 A.M. of a hot summer's night, and he was sitting in the open window reading in the paper about his own affidavit, when Bridgey Webber, a well-known gangster, put a hand on his shoulder. "Hello, Herman," said Bridgey in a loud voice, identifying the seated man beyond any possible doubt.

A very short time later, as Rosenthal stood on the steps of the restaurant about to leave, he was shot and killed by four hired murderers.

"Well, he got his!" was the verdict of the underworld.

Bald, slant-eyed Jack Rose, notorious gambler and procurer, turned state's evidence. The auto which drove up to the Metropole and discharged the four men was his. Lt. Charles Becker had ordered him to have Rosenthal put out of the way, threatening to frame *him* if he did not. So Jack got the four thugs and they had done the job: Lefty Louis, Dago Frank, Whitey Lewis and Gyp the Blood.

The names are burned into my memory. The restaurant was there for years, but under new management. Whitman became governor, and a reform mayor; John Purroy Mitchel (for whom I later worked) tried to clean up New York. But the Rosenthal case remained an indelible part of the Broadway story.

In New York you almost have to live more than one life, and that year I was living three lives simultaneously. How we did so much, working all day and playing half the night, I don't know. I remember how sleepy I often used to be. But I have scarcely forgotten a tune, or a face, or a street, or the name of a single play. (The fact that I never throw away a theater program helps.)

VII

NEW YORK—
SMALL SCALE

A change came almost overnight. Carefreeness flew out the window, and responsibility took over: I got married.

Strange as it may seem we girls were not marriage-minded in those particular years. Or perhaps it was only girls of our particular stamp, who had stepped out of the circumspect life of small-minded, mild-mannered communities and found ourselves in the dash and whirl of a metropolis. On Grove Street we had none of the college-dormitory talk about the ideal husband, or what we'd wear that first morning for breakfast. One of my Village roommates stated that if Alfred were one inch taller and one year older she might consider him—which is about as serious as any of us got. We were busy and independent, young and gay, and our relations with the men around us were comradely to a degree almost inconceivable today—from what one hears and reads. Above all, we were away from home and free of the prodding of ambitious or worried parents. The loss of my own father and mother, who had died within two years of each other, had left a shadow on my innermost being unacknowledged for many years, but the sadness of it was mitigated by the immediate excitement into which I had been thrown.

The change was not in sentiment, because before we were married Harry and I had shared Bohemia. But suddenly—after his declaration beside the right lion in front of the Public Library, and my own surprised but delighted acquiescence—we found ourselves hand in hand for what turned out to be a very long road ahead.

The two years just passed must surely have done something to quicken the perceptions of the migrant from New England—the sparkle of lively minds at George's Little House, the warm affection of the lost children, and the stirring social conscience of Bohemia. If nothing else, they combined to banish complacency for all time. Now the stature of the man at my side was to strengthen and deepen the outlook—if it could be done. If it were possible . . .

All through that year on Grove Street we had eaten together night after night at Polly's. We had wandered the narrow streets of the Village even after the saloons had emptied their human debris. New York was safe those days, and the drunks politely made way for us to pass. We had gone together to the theater.

When we saw Forbes-Robertson in *Hamlet*, Harry said, "We must go to *every* Hamlet!" And so we have. We have seen all the Hamlets—John Barrymore and Michael Strange, Basil Sydney in modern dress, Fritz Lieber and Ben Greet, the delight of students; Gielgud, Evans, Olivier,

Leslie Howard, down to Donald Madden in 1961 at the Phoenix on Second Avenue. The only one we passed up was Sarah Bernhardt, who was old enough at that point to have known better.

Harry already had close ties with the theater. His best friend was a drama critic, which meant free seats, and also a temporary theatrical job. When Mme. Vera Kamisarzhevsky, the famous Russian star, came over to New York in 1908 he found himself in the position of her publicity agent. Though neither actress nor agent knew a word of the other's language, they had a notable success. For three weeks Kamisarzhevsky played Russian repertory at Daly's Theater to sold-out houses that knew no Russian, and the press was ecstatic.

Besides this heady experience, in those days the young man was writing plays himself which he still looks back on with a sigh. But after we were married the theater receded to its proper niche outside real life, and our visits to the Liberal Club became fewer. It was no longer *over* but *down* to Polly's. Almost imperceptibly we had moved into the ranks of uptowners whom Bohemia forgot. Our lives took on a conformity and conventionality of which we took little notice at the time but which gradually set our feet in an entirely new direction. Besides this, our budget, while quite adequate, took planning. The rent money lay in the front left corner of the bottom drawer of the chiffonier under the underwear. This chiffonier was part of the five-piece cream-colored bedroom suite which was *de rigueur* for every newly-wed couple of that particular decade. I still have the chiffonier, and I still have a distinct respect for its banking facilities—for the comfort and security of knowing that that forty dollars was right where one could touch it.

The details of housekeeping became immediately absorbing. It may be that the bride of today has just as many demands, but I doubt if she gives herself up to them quite so wholeheartedly as we did then. The world is too close these days, what with radio and TV spinning their webs of fear and worry. Of what importance shelf paper in the face of nuclear war, segregation and superjets?

In those days we were "playing house." Marketing was a measure of thrift. One made daily trips to the food stores on uptown Broadway, mingling with the middle-aged bourgeois housewives who had been doing it for years, listening to their comments, watching the butcher with a sharp eye as he trimmed the meat before weighing it, trying to look wise. But you didn't fool that butcher. "How are?" was his regular greeting. His grin was a wide welcome even if he was saving with words. With no show of pedantry he taught me all I know about meat: where to pinch a chicken; when not to buy lamb; which good fatty streaks to look for in beef; how to recognize that delicate point in age when meat is old enough to be tender, yet not over the edge. "That's the way they like it in London," he assured me, holding up a rib roast dripping mold. It's something I've often pondered. He said that our best beef was sent over to England where they appreciated it, yet in the course of a long lifetime interspersed with travel, I have found the beef in London far from notable. But I'm sure he knew. After all, the steer he was holding up had been slaughtered before we entered World War I . . .

Our grocer was an Irishman named Phil. Phil was a fast add-er, and it was no use trying to keep up with him as his pencil flew down the long list of figures on the paper bag. I was completely confident of his honesty and of his adding ability, but I wanted to test my own and always hurried down the column along with him. Even now when I'm adding a bridge score I think of Phil and silently thank him. It's as long ago as 1925 that I last traded with him, but only a few months ago he sent his regards to me through a friend who still lives in the neighborhood where we were brides together. It was a voice from another planet.

Nick, the Greek fruit man, was expensive. Usually I went to one of the big markets where fruit and vegetables were cheaper—*big* but a far cry from today's supermarkets. There I would turn the strawberry basket upside down to see if any inferior berries were being put over on me, smell each apple, insist that the water be shaken from the spinach before it was weighed. Outrageous behavior it was, I realize now, but all part of an act designed to fool myself that I was in way of becoming a good housekeeper. Only for occasional luxuries did I go to Nick—apricots, grapes, persimmons, ripe figs from the Old Country!—and this I continued to do long after I moved away to another part of the city. Nick must have taken my marketing duplicity in his stride because we always were friends, and in our later days he introduced me by letter to his brother, whom we visited in Corinth.

Those first essays in buying left deep convictions. For years I not only went back to Nick from across the city, but when I want flowers for very special occasions I still order them from the florist next door to Nick. And I remember the tailor at 107th and Broadway with warmth and gratitude as an exceptional craftsman.

Shopping, which meant a trip downtown, accounted for afternoons of deep concentration. The West Side subway made a beeline for Macy's, and in twenty minutes one emerged from the dead air below ground to sunshine, rain or wind, and the busiest corner in New York. Shopping may seem irksome to some. Nowadays it seems so to me. But then it was titillating. You looked over the counters for markdowns, remnants, bargains. You tortured yourself

with indecision. You got fabric samples, made a trip back
home to try them out, another trip back to Macy's, and before finally deciding, to another store.

Fingering the elegant clothes which hung on racks at
the end of each season in stores other than Macy's was a
sensation, but one didn't give in to temptation. Trying on
hats was endless in a day when hats had sizes and 22½
was hard to find. Hours drifted by deliciously, and suddenly it was five o'clock; the subway was a solid mass of
humans. You had to push and be pushed to get in, twist
and be twisted to get out from among them. With supper
ahead to be cooked.

Time was *almost* endless and energy was inexhaust-
ible. Sometimes now I ride up the escalator at Macy's and
look out over the women and girls trying on hats, picking
at goods-by-the-yard, frowning thoughtfully at china cups,
and I wish I could still care that much. Wish I could lose
myself so as to forget the world.

Moving in New York was regulation. And by moving
I mean actually changing the locale of one's home. In those
palmy days apartments abounded, and the landlord had to
work to get you. He "decorated" for you every year: he
whitewashed the ceilings, varnished the floors and slab-
bered fresh paint on last year's unwashed paint. He papered
walls with paper of your own choice provided it came
within his price range, which meant that you saw the same
paper on the walls of all your friends' apartments. He frequently made concessions, offering one month's free rent,
two months' free rent, and leases were rarely for more than
one year.

It seemed almost easier to move than to stay. You
could skip house-cleaning, you told yourself, and avoid
having a painter pile up your furniture in the middle of

each room for a week and never unpile it. Instead, you
argued, you could walk straight into an interesting new
apartment, clean and freshly decorated.

Looking for apartments became a popular summer
sport. You picked the neighborhood you liked and walked
slowly through the streets looking for "For Rent" signs.
You asked to see apartments that were way beyond your
limit, just for thrills. And the dim closed-up large-roomed
apartments, opened up by a shuffling janitor, would be rich
with heavy rugs and tapestry-covered furniture, lamps of
dark Tiffany glass hanging low over dining-room tables,
the stuff of novels. They weren't your style, but they gave
a peep into another kind of life. You wondered about the
people who were at ease in that stuffy grandeur, and
glanced surreptitiously at framed photographs.

Forty dollars was a medium rent. Sixty dollars was
big but conceivable. More than sixty denoted a life of
which you had no part. So back in your own price range
the drama continued, still with accompanying excitement,
still with new combinations of rooms to be had, new ar-
rangements for furniture to consider, and the emergence
of a slightly aberrant household personality.

During those weeks you thought of little else.

Moving day was practically a New York holiday.
From the night of September 30 to the morning of October
2, side streets were lined with vans. Jobbers sometimes
moved two and three apartments in the one day. They'd
dump your furniture, and disappear to the next job. They
were all of a kind, men of brawn and beery breaths, ex-
stevedores or bar-bouncers. A week before their arrival the
husband-and-wife team spent each evening wrapping newspapers around china and glass, arranging them with ut-
most care in barrels, in order to withstand the dropping and
pushing they were surely going to get.

Nor was the actual moving the primrose path that you
tried to tell yourself it would be. The decorating job could
be done ahead only if the retiring tenant had in turn found
an apartment that he could get into before moving day.
Otherwise there would be the clash of your household arriving and his household departing. And once you were
installed in new quarters the same wheel once more started
to revolve. Curtains had to be lengthened or shortened, and
new ones bought for the extra window. The bathroom mats
didn't fit. (Once we had a triangular bathroom.) You
needed a new table for a chair. A new lamp for the new
table. Trips to Macy's began with renewed vigor, all other
householders doing the same, the stores as busy and almost
as full as before Christmas. You stood behind salesgirls,
goods in hand, watching your turn, ready to pounce.

Between 1914 and 1922 we moved six times—into
six new apartments of no perceptible difference one from
the other.

Instead of matinées we now went to the Polo Grounds
on Saturday afternoons to root for the Giants in their striped
suits. We watched for Catcher Chief Bender, a full-blooded
Indian whom the fans always greeted with the war cry. We
saw Connie Mack's Million-Dollar-Infield from Philadelphia
(Eddie Collins is the only one whose name I remember),
and Ty Cobb at the top of his fame with the Detroit Tigers.

It was at the Polo Grounds that the man from Fitchburg came over to greet my husband and me—the one who
told us about my father's baseball prowess. He was an
ex-mayor of Fitchburg, not unlike New York's Jimmy
Walker (of future date), good-looking, smartly dressed,
affable. That the Irish contingent from whom I sprang
were on the sporty side, I had accepted with mild disfavor
when I lived in New England. But my values were fast

changing. From time to time through years of World Series in New York several of these men have turned up, good company, all of them, jaunty, sophisticated, and a revelation to me who really had not known them at all. The ex-mayor also reminded me that Pat Moran, famous manager of the Phillies and later of the pennant-winning Cincinnati Reds, was a cousin of my Moran-Kielty grandmother. This relationship I had accepted vaguely in the past without pride. But when I went to look at Fitchburg once again in 1962, I went out to see the monument erected to Pat Moran in West Fitchburg where he was born, and meditated briefly on what a silly little snob I had once been.

In spring the hurdy-gurdy man—at first with monkey, and later, by rule of the S.P.C.A., without—ground out "Sancta Lucia" and "Funiculi-Funicula" for pennies. For many years it was the same shabby old man with a long drooping mustache. He must have walked many miles every week because I used to see him in all corners of the city. The last of a long, long line, he was finally put off the streets by Mayor La Guardia, who wasn't a man to stand for any nonsense. Since his time we've had no hurdy-gurdies.

On holidays German bands played in the courtyards of apartment houses, loud and, it seemed, deliberately off key. Far from throwing out pennies, we closed the windows.

Frequently in those days we took the subway to Borough Hall, Brooklyn, to visit friends who lived on the Heights, that oasis of wide streets, Civil War houses, dignity and peacefulness. The Heights is still spacious and beautiful, but the approach has changed almost beyond belief. In 1963 we returned to Borough Hall by subway after an absence of many years. Emerging into the daylight, into what used to be a hodgepodge of dark streets, gloomy buildings and an anarchy of traffic, we found ourselves in a vast open plaza, paved in light stone that shone in the midday sun, and for the first time we saw Borough Hall itself in proper perspective.—Once in the old days our friends told us about watching a rookie policeman trying to untangle the snarl of traffic at that spot—the worst in all of Greater New York. Horns tooted, cabbies shouted, cars were at a standstill. As they watched, our friends saw that the tall young cop was crying.

There are tricks for re-living the past. One way to recapture that particular small-scale New York is to take a ride on the IRT local subway south from Grand Central. This is the old section. The stations used to be dim and now they are flooded with light. The old turnstiles are gone, the fare has risen. But they *feel* the same. The station names stare out old and familiar, the insignia in careful tiling, a specific design for each station, far more imaginative than the functional signs used in the "new" subway. The same kind of people are riding, gum-chewing, tabloid-reading. The clothes are a bit more casual, men's top coats are short (among subway riders), pants are narrower, shoes are better. There is a mite less smell than when those Ukrainian peasants from Rivington Street used to get on at Grand Street—so strong that it carried you right back to the steppes. Fewer bearded Jews in double-breasted black coats are reading the worn volume of the Torah. When I was on jury duty not long ago, taking the local from Fourteenth Street down, I was back in the old days.

Besides the subway, four noisy El lines clattered up and down the city in those days—on Ninth, Sixth, Third and Second avenues. The Ninth went down Columbus

Avenue through Hell's Kitchen, past the lush fragrance of
chocolate factories in the Thirties, and on into dark turgid
Greenwich Street, parallel to the docks. Below it, saloons
and brothels beckoned, into which the sailors hurried, and
out of which they staggered, saturated. (Here for a time
was the hangout of Eugene O'Neill.) It was not a pleasant
ride.

The Sixth Avenue branched off the Ninth Avenue
tracks at Fifty-third Street and, on its way downtown,
skirted the theaters. It was Main Street for chorus girls,
stagehands, waiters. In open windows of three-story flats,
canary cages were hanging. At Forty-third the El passed
over Jack's, famous hangout for newsmen and stage folk,
immortalized by Samuel Hopkins Adams in *Tenderloin.*
At Twenty-seventh Street it went over Mouquin's, one of
the famous old French restaurants, formerly meeting place
of the sporty set, later the rendezvous of the foremost painters of the day, the so-called Ash Can Group—Maurice
Prendergast, William Glackens, George Luks, John Sloan,
Ernest Lawson, and the rest.

The Third Avenue El took you practically into the
tenements. Women leaned out over the window sills, children played on fire escapes. When the train slowed up you
sometimes witnessed a scene of domestic ferment. Clanging
loosely along over the dark cavern of a thoroughfare already spiritually darkened, on its way to the Tombs or City
Hall or Brooklyn Bridge, it still was not depressing as was
the Ninth Avenue El, not so secret and furtive. It caught
the eye of artists. You see it in the paintings of John Sloan
at the turn of the century, and of Edward Hopper a generation later. Long after the other lines had folded, the Third
Avenue El remained, its stations cozy right up to the end of
1955, Gothic overhangs decorating the roofs, wooden
benches with curved backs, and pot-bellied stoves that were
kept burning brightly in the winter.

The Third Avenue El sheltered and protected the Bowery and the Bowery bums. Even now, with their dark wing-cover removed, the tattered old men are still there. You see them leaning against the same old buildings, many of which are also still miraculously standing. They ask little of life—nothing more than a place to lie down and a little to eat, for both of which they are willing to queue up for hours, and enough to drink. They don't want jobs. They don't want women, it's said. They're not even what is known generally as "alcoholics." The Bowery bum, they say, is a social drinker. He seldom drinks alone, he'll pass the bottle, and combine with others to get the price of one. Even now, with its shadows brushed away and a plan afoot to modernize and socialize the Bowery, the thin pale men in old clothes continue to resist the light. There are said to be from twelve thousand to twenty thousand of them still around—looking just the same today as the gaunt figures one saw there in 1914, 1915, 1916—and before. We often walked from Grand Street to Chinatown for dinner. Or from Chinatown down Park Row to the Brooklyn Bridge and over the bridge, one of the loveliest walks in New York, then and now. The Bowery men took no notice then. Nor do they now.

A web of streetcars ran all over town in those days, and the Fifth Avenue buses had open tops which made for a perfect view of the city—along windy Riverside Drive, down Fifth Avenue-of-the-mansions, contemptuous then of apartment dwellers, through commercial Fifth Avenue lined with the most elegant shops in the world, and on to Washington Square and Stanford White's beautiful Arch.

Only a few skyscrapers thrust their towers aloft in 1914. The Singer Building (forty-one stories) was the only one I remember from my fairyland visit of 1908. The Woolworth Tower, built a few years later, was breathtaking. People rode down in the subway to City Hall just to get out and stare up at the "Cathedral" of commerce. Designed by Cass Gilbert and inspired by the London Houses of Parliament, it cost $13,500,000 for which it is said that the five-and-ten-cent-store magnate paid cash. The Flatiron Building was always good for a laugh—"twenty-three skiddoo"—girls' skirts ballooning in the wind at its sharp corner. It had no glamor. But opposite it the Metropolitan Life building was a thing of beauty. The Eternal Light caught the imagination, and Madison Square set it off with its big shade trees and the O. Henry characters resting under them.

One of the most striking earmarks of this new life was the interweaving of Jews into the overall pattern. I married a Jew, I was living in a city the background of which was dark-haired, bright-eyed, short-statured, in contrast to the big wide-faced Irish that was Boston. This city screen of New York was Italian as well as Jewish, but from the very first it was the Jews with whom I had a special affiliation. With my H.S.G.S. indoctrination I was always more expert than Harry at picking a Jewish figure in a crowd— the counterpart of some child whose face I had come to know well. I would see the brothers or uncles or cousins of these children in the subway, at the theater, behind delicatessen counters. But more important were the many individual friendships enkindled in those early days. Few people, I claim, have had such a unique opportunity to know so many Jewish figures from so many backgrounds, with such varieties in living, in taste and interests. There they were awaiting me when I emerged from my adolescent cocoon—the Weisses, the wits in George's Little House, school children, housemothers, and now families, friends,

shopkeepers—smart intrepid people whom, God forbid, I
might never have come to know had I stayed on in Fitchburg. There they were strange to me, here they were my
familiars.

We were all so guileless, back there in 1914! Our
pleasures were simple and our energies devoted to small
immediate needs. If we thought about such a generality at
all, we'd say that, yes, we were secure. Politics had little
interest for most of us, and Europe was the stuff of novels.
When the upheaval of war shook the foundations of our
world, we were as unprepared for it as children.

To a young couple just married with a home to make
and life in a big city to adjust to, war in Europe was far-off
drama. It made fascinating reading, but was hardly more
than incidental in daily living. Through that lovely week in
midsummer, 1914—I remember the weather vividly—
when the first news began to come through, people gathered around newsstands to read the headlines: Austria declaring war on Serbia (July 28); Germany declaring war
on Russia (August 1); Germany declaring war on France
(August 3); Belgium overrun and Britain declaring war
on Germany (August 2). The air at night was filled with
"Extra! Extra!" shouted by newsboys, and everywhere men
came down out of their houses, pennies in hand. I was doing social work at that time and saw a fist fight in Yorkville
in the bakery where I was having lunch. Pro-Germans
around New York were nearly as numerous as Pro-English.
People put maps on their walls, and in time, as the war ad-
vanced, stuck pins in to show the movement of troops. We
trusted Woodrow Wilson "to keep us out of the war." We
also wanted the "world made safe for democracy." But none
of these slogans touched us emotionally.

When America got in we felt the impact, but only slightly more than before. Many of our friends were signing up. Young married men, especially those with children or children expected, were exempt. We were safe. But for years afterward I felt that by my very existence I had stood between my young husband and the Big Adventure. And he, I think, would have liked the chance to go.

For the 1914 war *was* Big Adventure. It was romantic and sentimental. As the awful descriptions of Verdun came to be printed in the newspapers, and the casualties of English and French youth piled up, it became tragedy, but tragedy of high order, tinged with heroic patriotism. The trenches, the mud, the rats, the lice, the unspeakable horrors which we read about with such avid curiosity, we did not really grasp. It was too remote in every way from our home and our experience. On the other hand, we thrilled over officers from France in light blue, English in khaki and Sam Brown belts, Anzacs in wide turned-up hats—common sights along Fifth Avenue. We spoke glowingly of "poilus" and "tommies" and "doughboys." Canteens were scattered along the Hudson for incoming sailors, with dances and shows, and every girl, wife, and mother who could possibly get away, waited on tables and did her bit to the tune of "K-K-K-Katy, Beautiful Katy" and "How Ya Gonna Keep 'em Down on the Farm?" For anyone who was by way of becoming an adult during those years, the war songs of 1914-18 still send a shiver down the spine—a sudden sharp pang of nostalgia. The present drops away. "Pack Up Your Troubles in Your Old Kitbag and Smile, Smile, Smile" . . . "There's a Long, Long Trail . . ." It is our youth that we are remembering.

For the boys themselves, our soldiers of the Great War who went Over There, it was also drama of the first order. Unlike the boys of World War II who close their minds to what they did in four blank years, trying to forget, those earlier ones remained soldier boys. They still have their reunions, reminisce about their life in Paris and the trenches, sing their songs.

Armistice Day was like no other day in all history.

The entire city went out on the streets and cried and danced and sang for joy. The relief was unbelievable. Without realizing it we had been under constant tension, I suppose, and of a sudden the potential danger was gone, the lurking fear. It was OVER—the war that seemed to have been with us all our lives!

The bugles on the battlefields had sounded their "Cease Fire" at 11 A.M. European time, November 11. In New York the news slipped out into Times Square before daylight. Milkmen heard about it first—in that day before radio; then policemen, and night workers going home. Quite early in the morning a girl climbed up on the platform at Broadway and Seventh Avenue that had been erected for selling Liberty Bonds, and there sang the doxology—"Praise God from Whom all Blessings Flow." The gathered crowd listened reverently, many kneeling. She then sang the "Marseillaise" and "The Star-Spangled Banner" and "God Save the King."

Bells pealed throughout the city all day. Autos back-fired raucously. Offices closed, schools closed, banks, factories. The porters in Grand Central Station marched single-file through the station carrying their service flag which had two gold stars for those who had been killed in action. (I remember in later years seeing the long grim list of the dead in every bank and store and railroad station in France and England.)

At night the ships on the Hudson played their search-lights up and down Riverside Drive, and everybody was out in the streets who could get there. Coincident with victory was the epidemic of Spanish flu, and my unfortunate Harry, who had it, was still in bed. Though his fever was gone he could not join in the festivities, so we opened the window, the better to hear the joyous noise, and the searchlights from the Hudson shot into our very room. But I saw Times Square, with my friend Molly, and Times Square was in a frenzy. Strangers kissed. Wounded soldiers and sailors from Ellis Island Military Hospital were brought over and stationed in front of the Astor where they could see it all. Girls danced rings around them. It was carnival, but with no rowdiness. The police were tact itself, never letting the celebration get out of hand, but joining in and encouraging it.

We were onlookers, Molly and I, as we were so often to be onlookers together during the years to come. But our hearts were singing and rejoicing with the mob that milled up and down Broadway.

What was true of New York was apparently true of Paris and London. Never in all the world's history, before or since, has so large a number of the human race thrilled simultaneously with the same emotion from the same cause.

Months later when the 77th Division returned from France we were at Madison Square and Twenty-sixth Street at 7 A.M., Harry and Molly and I, standing on the steps of Park & Tilford's store, waiting to see New York's Own march triumphantly up Fifth Avenue in their khaki puttees. Again our hearts beat fast at waving flags and playing bands and the tread of marching feet. It was the last scene of an operetta!

In four years fourteen million men were killed or badly wounded or forever broken of nerve. In one single battle the British lost nearly half a million men. A second lieutenant's average expectancy of life in the trenches was a fortnight. When we were in London in 1922, and commented on how very few men one saw in the theaters, the answer was, "They're all dead!" The empire under which so much of our world had basked with so much serenity for generations—even if vicariously—was already toppling. The toboggan slide of civilization had started.

It was years later, in 1962, after reading *The Guns of August*, by Barbara Tuchman, that I was finally able to comprehend the magnitude of the period through which most of us who were young had so innocently passed. Harry had followed the movements of armies as he would have followed a football match. He watched intelligently. Six years after the war he was able to point out the strategy of the opposing troops to a busload of tourists doing the battlefields, where the young French guide was floundering. But though I lived through it beside him, the war never touched me. Now, in 1962, I was finally confronted with the reality of those cataclysmic years. Never mind if it was military history, and if these were figures out of the world of great events, this historical book was my past too. It was *my* personal document, which I read with shocked attention. Names came back out of the past: von Moltke, Haig, Foch, the Kaiser (was he ridiculous or was he sinister?), the Crown Prince (was he simple or worse?), Papa Joffre with his drooping white mustache . . . I hadn't known much about what they stood for, but certain aspects of their personalities had penetrated and cut far deeper in memory than any figures of the world-shaking periods that have come since or came earlier. Now, however, I saw them as men for the first time. Old men and stupid men and over-ambitious, whose fatal misjudgments had hurled us into the grand climax of history through which we had somehow lived. Also those who were not so stupid or heartless:

the Grand Duke of all the Russians, who wept when he
was made commander-in-chief of the Russian armies—
wept for himself and for Russia; the French Minister of
War, Messimy, opening a Cabinet meeting on August 5
with a speech full of valor and confidence, who broke off
midway, buried his head in his hands and sobbed; Winston
Churchill, wishing godspeed and victory to the BEF, who
broke down and cried so that he could not finish the sen-
tence. And Sir Edward Grey, looking out through the window of Whitehall at London: "The lamps are going out
all over Europe; we shall not see them lit again in our lifetime." . . . There were some in 1914 who sensed the
tragedy—for themselves, but more for their countries and
for all the world.

Another revelation that the perspective of time has
disclosed is how so many component factors in the history
of the next fifty years began to fall into place at that time.
A rift was created in the ranks of thinking Americans that
was to widen and deepen in the decades to come. The intellegentsia of the World War I days were largely pacifists.
"The war is a clash of traders!" cried Jack Reed, who
wasn't so much a pacifist as a romantic whose idea of fighting meant the wild forays of Mexico's Pancho Villa, which
he had covered for the *Metropolitan* magazine.

In 1916 when Woodrow Wilson was running for a
second term the liberals stood solidly behind him. An appeal was signed by Lincoln Steffens, George Cram Cook,
Susan Glaspell, Hutchins Hapgood, Zona Gale and dozens
of others of the old-line intellectuals, to vote for Wilson
"because he kept us out of war." But in April, 1917, when
they found their country lined up on the Allied side prepared to fight in Europe, their fury knew no bounds: *they
had been double-crossed*.

Their eyes now turned toward Russia. Russia had eliminated herself from the war, thrown out the Czar and started a revolution. Jack Reed got an assignment to go there, he died there, he became a symbol. Lincoln Steffens went over and wrote back, "I have seen the future, and it works!"

But the far-reaching significance of these events for the decades to come we could never have possibly imagined in that last year of the war, or on Armistice Day when there was dancing in the streets. Bohemia, if we thought of it at all, took on the aspect of an isolated outpost.

VIII

THE TWENTIES

It was at least four years after the Great War that the Golden Age began to shine. That there was a depression in-between I remember chiefly because in 1921 we moved into a somewhat smaller instead of a somewhat larger apartment. We were a family now. Whether we chose to or not we had to live a fairly circumspect life. But we were not unaffected by the shimmer around us. Hard times quickly receded, our own income began gradually to rise, and the extravagant playfulness of a reckless age took over. To have lived through the twenties in New York was a special experience, and to those of us who were young, the middle years of that decade churned up unprecedented excitement. In spite of the questionable philosophy current and some of the disastrous happenings, we loved it. What went on didn't seem tawdry then. It was amusing.

As an informed public we had every reason to be cynical throughout those years. The New York *World* saw to that. Each morning we were presented with the political scandals of Tea Pot Dome, the debacle of the United States in the League of Nations, the slaughter of law and order that came with Prohibition, the names of bootleggers, gangsters, racketeers. No one needed to be deceived. But few were willing to concern themselves with the decay in government and elsewhere. The war was over and we were tired of Causes.

How much of this moral indolence was a psychological reaction to war and events, and how much to easy money and the consumption of gin, is questionable. General drinking was something new in the 1920's. Smart young city folks led the fashion, and their counterparts in ever widening circles around the country echoed them. Not everyone was affected. My New England friends seemed immune to the trend. But on the whole the U.S.A. took to drink. People who had never had a cocktail now drank catgut gin that would have burned away their throats without the orange-juice mixture that made it relatively smooth. (I know a flapper of that day, now in her sixties, who still carries her own little bottle of orange juice to every party.)

Speakeasies were a superficially attractive Prohibition institution. Up a flight, down a flight, in a backroom, always with an air of secrecy that deceived no one, they were far from sinister. In fact they were rather snug, and more fun than restaurants were before or have been since. People talked easily, probably much as in the old-time saloon and pub, said to have been so comforting to the workingman. The speakeasy habitués were in no need of comfort, but they enjoyed the sociability. I don't remember seeing sodden drunks. But they must have been around: according to statistics, in 1926 alone two thousand violators of the law died of poison liquor.

Then there was Flaming Youth, girls fresh out of school swishing short skirts and smoking their first cigarettes. It's not news now for skirts to shoot up from ankles to knees, but it was a shock then. Stockings, which had been black or white or brown, suddenly took on pale flesh tones, the better to show off the new expanse of fine long legs. I saw beige silk stockings for the first time in Paris in 1922 and was sufficiently impressed to write home about them. Make-up, which up to then (except for a light dust of powder) had been the hallmark of the cheap and "unrefined," and since has come into the category of a minor art, was smeared on. There were no subtleties. Girls were out frankly to allure.

Falling in love, passionately, abysmally, throwing discretion to the wind, was the theme of verse and story—Dorothy Parker's couplets, Kay Brush's *Young Man of Manhattan*, Iris March in *The Green Hat*. The torch song echoed in the hearts of philanderers. "Mon Homme"—a deserted girl leaning futilely against a lamppost. "Moanin' Low . . ."

The Gray-Snyder murder was one of the ugliest manifestations of the time: the big blond housewife, Ruth Snyder, and her mild husband, living in one of the rows upon rows of all-alike frame houses that stretch as far as the eye can reach in Queens; the ebullient corset salesman, Judd Gray; the insurance money and the seven abortive attempts Ruth made on her husband's life before the final success with window cord, sash weights and Judd's help.

I remember two magnificent girls who were just as much the victims of false values. It was at a party on Central Park South overlooking the twinkling lights of the park that I first saw them. They came in together, both taller than average, their height crowned with big shako-type fur hats, one of soft black lynx, the other of blond fox.

They were not showgirls. In another day and age they would have been classed as "ladies," but in 1926 no girl wanted to be called a "lady." A few years later one of these girls put on a white evening dress, silver slippers and an ermine wrap, went into the garage and turned on the gas. She died in the height of her beauty, at thirty-three. The other jumped out of a hotel window very near to the party spot where we had met them.

Starr Faithful was still another, a speakeasy girl, man-mad, drink-mad, a beautiful young woman who hadn't a chance from the first, whose body was washed up on the Long Island shore, and whose only immortality was the stream of scandal that ran through the courts and the newspapers.

But we did laugh a lot in those crazy days. Shows were funny and parties were gay. Nowadays in the theater there is wit. You smile, chuckle, roll an allusion around on your tongue. But there aren't many guffaws. The playhouse doesn't rock with the roars of laughter as it used to. I remember Harry laughing so hard that he could scarcely catch his breath, tears rolling down his cheeks: W. C. Fields at the billiard table, with his spongy face and overblown nose . . . Fields playing golf, noncommittal and expressionless . . . Fields mincing about on a croquet lawn. There were Ed Wynn, Eddie Cantor, Bert Williams, Will Rogers, the Marx Brothers, all tucked away in the interstices of the Follies. Ziegfeld allowed comedy acts only to give the girls time to change their costumes, and the Follies girls were not funny, heaven forbid! They were *magnifique*, elongated, disdainful, sweeping down marble stairways designed by Joseph Urban, gowns by Lucille.

It seems far away now. But some of the girls are still around. Many of them married well; several, it's said, made good on Wall Street tips; and rich and poor alike turn up for the annual Ziegfeld Club ball. Marion Davies, we all know, became a multimillionaire; and Dr. Justine Johnstone, her friend, rival and co-star, won renown in a science laboratory in California. I sometimes see one of the famous beauties in a certain Broadway restaurant where she is now head checkroom girl, easy-going in middle age, greeting the current Broadway great with a casual wave. I have also seen Ann Pennington more than once, dancer of the Black Bottom, whose celebrated knees were considered the most beautiful in the world. I have seen her at the races, rather stout now, gray-haired, eyes on her chart, engrossed in the business of the day.

Parties were gay. To a girl from Fitchburg, with a brief interim of intellectual intensity behind her and house-wifery her chosen career, they were unforgettable. One of the first we went to in those glittering days was held at the House of Flowers. It seems odd. But what could be a more entrancing setting for a party than the greenery of a fine florist shop! This was a late party, with abundant food, a dance orchestra, and Governor Al Smith as guest of honor. He was easy to talk to, full of stories. Most of the time he sat at a table with a group of middle-aged cronies, highballs in hand. I don't think anyone else at the party held a glass. And I was just New England enough to be stunned to see a public official—indeed a governor!—drinking openly and casually when Prohibition was the law of the land. I didn't hold it against Al Smith. I didn't stand in judgment. I was just amazed.

But we got used to it. Another party was at the Brevoort. This was to honor a young state senator down from Albany who had just won repeal of the censorship bill. It was a dinner given by the civil liberties group, or an earlier equivalent, in celebration of this young liberal's hard fought, hard won success. His name was James J. Walker, and that night he was the darling of the intellegentsia. "I have never heard," said he, "of a girl being ruined by a book." At that party each table was provided with a pitcher of "iced tea."

The "literary tea" was the precursor of the ubiquitous cocktail party of today. At first publishers did serve tea, in their own shops, among the books. I remember such a party for A.E., the Irish poet, down among the Macmillan bookshelves on lower Fifth Avenue, and several at Alfred Knopf's office in the Heckscher Building. Random House was still serving tea when they gave a party for Gertrude Stein in their crowded quarters on Fifty-seventh Street. Later, however, publishers like everyone else added liquor, and finally omitted the tea and the cakes. Eventually they managed to avoid any taint of the literary.

I recall a gala affair at the newly opened Savoy-Plaza given for Richard Halliburton, slim young Princeton explorer who had one enormous success with *The Royal Road to Romance*, and was now celebrating *The Glorious Adventure*. He was everybody's hero. By this time there was no question about liquor. Martinis had taken over, the hors d'oeuvres covered a table that extended the length of the ballroom, a band played for dancing, and a quartet of heavy-set Negroes, dressed in pink satin suits with knee britches, sang close harmony.

Halliburton we knew only slightly and this was the last time we saw him, although it was ten years later that he went down in his Chinese junk in a typhoon off Midway Island in the Pacific. Or so the world thought. It was one of those unsolved mysteries.

Joan Lowell, author of *The Cradle of the Deep*, had a brief moment and a big party. The party was on board the *Ile de France*, everyone was there, opera hats, white tie, gloves to the shoulder, champagne. Her publishers gave the party, and her literary agent, one of the most respected and successful in the city, hovered protectively.

Joan was a rather plain, dark-haired bright-eyed girl. Her book was about her first sixteen years, spent entirely on a full-rigged schooner, the *Minnie A. Caine*, of which her father was captain, and on which she was the only female. She grew up to be part of the crew. She could reef and steer with the best of them, blaspheme and spit. Her first nightgown was a flour bag.

Joan was now the toast of the landlubbers. At the *Ile de France* party she couldn't have been more demure, with her smooth boyish bob and her short white chiffon dress, particularly titillating after the blue-jeans and sweat shirt in which the readers of her book pictured her. That the party was raided by prohibition agents, who picked up a bottle or two of liquor and charged the publisher seven dollars (paid on the spot), was only a shadow of the trouble that was to darken the publishers' office for a few weeks to come, and put Joan—at least temporarily—out of business as an author.

The book was published in March, 1929, and by April the truth was out. Instead of sixteen years at sea—"the only woman thing aboard"—it was discovered that Joan had spent part of one year only on board ship, and that with her were her mother, her sisters and her brothers. Her father commanded the *Minnie A. Caine*, but for only one year. And the grand climax—the fire so vividly described at the end which totally destroyed the vessel, all hands swimming for shore, Joan with a kitten clawing her shoulder—turned out to be a small dockside conflagration. At the time of publication the old *Minnie* was still in existence in an Australian backwash.

· · ·

Charles Studin's literary teas were unique. They were
held in his home on East Twelfth Street on Tuesday afternoons, and they went on for years. Charlie was a tall big-
boned man who at one time must have been heavy, but
dieting had thinned him down and left his jowls sagging.
He looked not unlike a sad friendly bloodhound, and like
that species he was kind and gentle. He had had a serious
illness and been told by his doctor to take it easy for the
rest of his life—the easier, the longer. So since he loved
life and people, he worked out a formula for combining
them and still conforming to the doctor's orders. Every
Tuesday he gave a tea which ended promptly at seven
o'clock, after which he went to bed. He gave them for a
new author, a college professor, a young actress, a poet, an
artist. If he were still alive he'd be giving them for astro-
nauts and biochemists. His backlog of regular guests
covered the field of the New York intelligentsia, though
least often did you see lawyers or businessmen, because
these were the ones with whom he spent his working days.
(He was a lawyer.) Of a Tuesday afternoon his two living
rooms were pretty consistently packed. If you accepted and
didn't show, Charlie was aware in spite of the mob, and
if you failed him twice without proper notice, you were
quite rightly crossed off the list.

Though these parties went on into the thirties, Prohibition was still on, and Charlie served liquor, not tea. He
himself was not allowed a drop of alcohol, his Filipino servant also did not drink, so they didn't know, and the result
was fantastic. They served only martinis, which the little
Filipino mixed early in the morning without tasting, all at
one time, and enough to last for a two-and-a-half-hour party
of anywhere from thirty to a hundred guests. There was
very little ice, if any. But everyone was there and holding

a glass, because no one really wanted to hurt Charlie, or lose his place on Charlie's list.

Today's solid publishers were then a group of gay young blades who prided themselves on their bachelorhood and played hard to get. I think they had a club—Bennett Cerf, Eugene Reynal, Marshall Best, Dick Simon, Max Schuster, George Oppenheimer, Dan Longwell . . .

Bennett Cerf lived with his father, Pop, at the Hotel Navarro, and gave good parties, the mixture literary and theatrical in about even proportions. There was always shop talk in corners and plenty of tunes in the air, with George Gershwin or Dick Rodgers at the piano; comparatively little drinking, delicatessen food, and an enormous Reuben's cheese cake.

Dick Simon lived with his father, too, in a brownstone on the West Side, with a family of three younger brothers and a still younger sister. All four boys were musical, two of them later took up music as a profession, and the two who went into publishing could have been stand-ins for their tunesmith brothers. What Dick liked best in those early days was to stay home, surrounded by his father and brothers and pretty little sister, with someone, usually Dick himself, at the piano. He became an amazingly successful publisher, but I always thought his heart remained in music. One of the last things Dick did before he died, I've heard, was to play piano duets with his brother Al.

When Dick and Max Schuster became publishing partners, getting their start with the famous crossword puzzle book, the music mystique spread to Max. Both men ate breakfast in their respective apartments, to records. One preferred Mozart, the other Beethoven, with his egg. Both were keen on symphonic literature. I recall one long cold drive of forty miles from New Jersey to New York in an open touring car. This was about 1928. Dick and Max sat

on the windy back seat, huddled together in a blanket, de-
fying the cold by singing the themes of Beethoven symphonies. They claimed they could go through all nine, and
by the time we got to Kearney they had indeed finished the
four movements of the First Symphony. We never heard
them through the remaining eight symphonies, but I have
no doubt they could have done it.

Those were high-stepping days. Reuben's (of the
cheesecake) was open all night, and filled all night. It was
a gathering place for talkers. One couple whom we knew
divided their time between an apartment in the city and a
house in Westchester. In the apartment they sometimes
gave dances, hired a red-hot jazz pianist, a Negro named
Hughie, pulled up the rugs and let the guests Charleston
through from room to room. One hot summer's night, when
they were out in their Westchester home, the girl complained that she was hungry and couldn't get her mind off
a Reuben's triple ham-and-chicken-on-rye. So her husband
picked up the telephone, ordered Reuben's to make up two
triple ham-and-chicken-on-rye and send them out to Harri-
son—pronto. Which they did. Reuben's still goes on. I
suppose it still stays open all night. But I wouldn't know.
Even then the waiters' feet were giving out, some of the
old ones walking on the sides of their shoes for relief.

Never was there a period of such sustained excitement. Everybody was on the crest. Everything was easy.
And when I look back upon my own audacity I am over-
come. On February 21, 1922, in a state of delirious exhilaration, I stepped blithely on board the old *Rochambeau* of
the French Line and took off with my friend Molly for
Paris.

It was a spree. Europe had been the background of

novels, then the background of war. Now it was to be ours.
The *Rochambeau*—dear to the hearts of all who crossed
on her in those long-ago days—rode the winter waves with
the ease of a whale at play. Her *salle à manger* was made
up of long wooden tables with racks to hold the plates. Her
passengers were like a family.

The *pension* where we stayed in Paris was on rue
Notre-Dame-des-Champs. It was a seedy small palace
which had originally housed the ladies-in-waiting on the
queen, accessible in those days by a short cut across the
fields to the Luxembourg. At ten o'clock sharp the gate
was locked and one had to ring a noisy bell to get into the
courtyard. Directly opposite was the Atelier de la Grande
Chaumière where, I've learned since, Renoir and Pissaro
and occasionally Cezanne painted in their young days. And
on the next corner, at the juncture of Boulevard Mont-
parnasse and Boulevard Raspail, was a cheerful-looking,
brightly lighted café.

One cold March evening we ventured in. The café was
noisy with laugh and talk, the crowd was young and gay,
on the whole poorly dressed, and eating in large groups
around tables to which any newcomer was welcome. Entirely by chance, and without ever having heard its name,
we had stepped into the Café Rotonde, at that time the
exact center of the art world. Paris in 1922 was like Greenwich Village in 1913, its artists and writers unknown, not
yet sure of themselves, not particularly self-conscious. It is
only in looking back that the period and the place have become epochal. That night and the many nights that followed, the Rotonde for us was just a warm crowded place,
its customers on the whole hard up and friendly. It could
be anywhere. But it wasn't. From our first unpremeditated
entrance we recognized that the air was electric.

This was the Paris of James Joyce and Ezra Pound,

Gertrude Stein and her early Picassos, Sylvia Beach in her Shakespeare and Company, that life-giving bookshop. Ernest Hemingway moved in the next year and lived farther along on the same rue Notre-Dame-des-Champs. That was long after we were gone. He was twenty-five, and had had only a book of short stories published that wasn't doing too well. He was poor, hard-working and happy, while Scott Fitzgerald, ensconced on the Right Bank with Zelda, was successful and already unhappy. In that one year the Rotonde seems to have changed. Its day of genuineness had waned. People began going there in order to show themselves. It was already banal.

All our lives Molly and I had fun together. She was original and adventurous, and a true wit. People said that she looked remarkably like Geraldine Farrar, with gray-green eyes, dark wavy hair, smiling bright face. Everybody liked her. I remember a small but characteristic incident when we were traveling. We had returned from the dining car to our seats in the second-class compartment, where there had been other passengers when we went out. Now they had all departed. But on the seat where Molly had sat was a paper with one word written: "*Simpático.*"

I was lucky to have such a good companion. Through a long life I have observed that a close woman friend is a rarity among married women after the first year or so of marriage, when college ties sometimes still lap over. By friend I don't mean a neighbor who drops in, or a bridge partner, or someone to go with to a matinée or lecture once a week. I mean a friend to whom you can talk with complete openness, and with whom you can be silent. Molly and I were each other's *alter ego*. We knew in general what the other's angle would be on nearly every question, but we wanted to hear it. And we wanted to report our own. She was a teacher of young children and delighted in her work.

Our friendship started in the stimulating atmosphere of George's Little House where she was one of the contingent that came out from New York for so many glorious Sundays. We had seen the Armistice together, and all through the twenties we lunched on Saturdays at the Algonquin. Just as at the Armistice we hadn't actually danced in the streets, so now we did not sit at the famous Round Table at the Algonquin, rendezvous of F.P.A., Bob Benchley, George Kaufman, Alec Woolcott, *et al.* We were on the side lines, and as I look back I think it was the best place to be. In later years, when Harry and I came to be a little more on the inside than in those carefree early days, I don't think it was quite so merry. Participation meant responsibility, awareness and a certain self-consciousness.

Sometime in the twenties I wrote a little book called *The Sidewalks of New York*, which was bought by the Bowman hotels (who used to run the Biltmore, the Commodore and other big transient hostelries) to give to their guests. I never could have written it had it not been for Molly, who first opened up the city to me. From 1913 on we prowled the byways of New York together every Saturday afternoon. After lunch we'd look up old streets and old houses, visit galleries, take tea at the Plaza or, on warm days, at Claremont Inn overlooking the Hudson. It was the perfect formula for a New York Saturday afternoon.

"If you're not happy, people don't want to be with you," I remember Molly saying once. In her last four years she was in almost constant agony, but people still wanted to be with her. She lived—characteristically—in the heart of the city, on West Fifty-fifth Street, and friends dropped in every day, not because they felt it a duty to the sick but because they enjoyed themselves being there.

Café Society was born in those years—a new social order. Based on a combination of Social Register and actors, dance-band leaders, newspaper columnists, publishers, editors, it was a letting down of social barriers that may have been induced by the war and the egalitarian aspect of the trenches. It was not a case of the entertainment world pushing its way in so much as society shaking loose from its fetters. On both sides the members were likely to be people of verve.

The Casino in Central Park was the glittering background of that special whirl, and Jimmy Walker, by then the dapper mayor of New York, its Beau. He played his part at first with dash, then with recklessness and ever increasing public disapprobation, winding up finally in social and political obliteration. But for two years, when the Casino was his favored milieu, it was the most elegant rendezvous of frivolous society. As a restaurant it ranked with the best in the Bois de Boulogne, which it resembled—a spacious white mansion in the middle of the park, with broad verandahs and candle-lighted tables. How well I remember sitting there on the night of a full moon, the music and laughter muted, and the scent of wisteria wafted over from the nearby terrace.

There were two dining rooms, each with décor by Joseph Urban reminiscent of the Follies—one lushly tropical, the other French. There were two orchestras, Leo Reisman's and his young disciple Eddy Duchin's. It was the day of "sweet " music sung yearningly by the saxophones: "In dreams I kiss your hand, Madame/Your dainty finger tips . . . I haven't any right, Madame/To do the things I do . . ." The Casino was dressy: diplomats with foreign ribbons across their white-bosomed shirts; Jimmy Walker impeccable in white tie and tails; Grover Whalen, the hand-shaker; the Harrimans, Averell and Marie; beautiful Rosamond Pinchot; blond green-eyed actress Miriam Hopkins; lissome Gertrude Lawrence; the Honorable Daisy Fellowes . . .

Eddy Duchin played piano like an angel. He played so well that Rachmaninoff used to go to a saloon (I think it was out in California that he did this) to hear him. In that good-looking graceful young age, Duchin had what someone called "unconscious class" . . . sitting at the piano . . . standing against a mantelpiece . . . strolling. In 1935 he married Marjorie Oelrichs, who was beautiful, rich and socially irreproachable until her marriage, after which she was dropped from the Register. She died in 1937, twenty-nine years old, shortly after giving birth to her son Peter. In 1962 Peter Duchin opened the season in the Maisonette Room at the St. Regis with his own orchestra, as his father had done before him at the Casino. But it is a different kind of music that modern New York demands. A harsher kind.

Prohibition went into effect January 1, 1920. Jimmy Walker was inaugurated mayor in January, 1926. The Casino was closed and padlocked in 1931, Walker resigned in September, 1932, the Repeal of Prohibition came off in December, 1933, and where the Casino stood, a children's playground was established by Mayor Fiorello La Guardia. Only the wisteria vine remains.

IX

FAMILY LIFE

We were now a family with two children, a boy Tom and a
girl Katharine. We had a maid-of-all-work, Susie, and an
apartment into which we finally settled for sixteen years.

As I look back, the most vital time—the time most
vividly remembered—seems to have been those days when
the children were in school, when we lived on Riverside
Drive and in Bernardsville, New Jersey, the days of Susie,
of Khaki, the dog, and Sabbie, the cat. Sabbie and Khaki
were personalities well known to our friends, and our inti-
mates were so close to Susie that they usually talked with
her at some length on the telephone before speaking to us.
We were a family unit, combining our energies in all our
activities—meals, games, trips, culture, friends.

Throughout the years when the world was going

mad, we were leading a physically healthy, all-encompassing life. We were rarely quiet, it is true. I sometimes dream now of a calmness which we might have had, but which we never achieved. The children went to a large school run by Columbia University, their friends went to the same school, and all lived within the confines of that university village which stretched from Riverside Drive to Morningside Drive, from 114th to 122nd streets. They skated on the flooded tennis courts near where Riverside Church now stands, and slid on the snowbanks to the tracks of the West Side New York Central.

Family life in New York was not so different from family life everywhere else. The children rushed off to school in the morning, played outdoors in the afternoon, had other children in and out of the house, did homework after dinner at night and practiced before breakfast. Father went to his work every morning and came home tired, Mother ran the house—in her way. There were likely to be outings on Saturday, and newspapers and a big noon meal on Sunday.

Some aspects of our children's doings were decidely urban. To what extent I didn't know myself until a few years ago when another mother told me about a game which she had seen them engaged in. She lived directly behind us on Claremont Avenue. This was up the hill from Riverside, so that our roof was on a level with her eye. What she saw was our two and two others, ten stories from the ground, jumping from our apartment house roof to the next.

I'd say that in all New York Riverside Drive was the ideal spot for a child to live. The sun set over the Palisades in glory. The river was alive with boats—low gray Navy vessels anchored so close that we could hear the bells of the watch and see the semaphore signals; graceful private yachts that occasionally drifted past; and tugs tooting busily all day long.

It was breezy on Riverside. So much so, that making the corner of 116th Street could be a challenge. You bent your body and pushed. Or sailed up, skirts whirling. The winter wind was so strong that even where our west windows were tightly closed, the curtains blew stiffly into the room. Guests sometimes kept on their coats, and hugged the fire. (We had a real fireplace, which was not common in those days.) Years after we were installed and knew the idiosyncrasies of Drive living, our old friend Whit Burnett and his wife Martha Foley moved up to Riverside from the low-lying region of Greenwich Village. The moving van managed to park outside the apartment house, but their furniture was swept off the sidewalk by the force of the wind, and one of the windows in their new flat blew in. "We knew Riverside Drive was windy," said Martha philosophically, in her civilized way, accepting nature as she found it, but at a loss. What no one realized was that at the very moment they were moving in, the hurricane of September, 1938, was breaking over the city.

Summers we were able to get out into the country— which helps. We took trips to Bear Mountain. At an early age the children jumped the big waves in the surf of a lonely Long Island beach, and later rode horseback in New Jersey. Back in the city we took them to the theater at a tender age, even to opera. They had a stiff schedule of homework as the years progressed, and took music lessons throughout the years. I don't know how they did it all, or what ill effects this highly stimulating program, imposed as it was upon them so young, may have had on their psyches.

But I do know who put them up to it. To cover so much ground and keep within the confines of time, I became a sort of circus ringmaster—planner, arranger for the broad overall scheme and the daily details of at least three out of our four lives (Harry was still pretty much out of my jurisdiction). But I never could have engineered it without Susie. Without her the life of our family would have been quite another story.

Susie came out of Ireland at the age of seventeen. But we did not know her until four years later when, in October, 1921, she turned up at our apartment in answer to an ad we ran in the "Help Wanted" section of the Sunday *Times*. "Wanted: general houseworker, sleep in, 2 children in family, $25 monthly." With address.

She was a sturdy-looking girl with black hair and bright rosy cheeks. I looked her over with a cool eye, as one could in those days, and she looked right back under heavy brows, ready to take up cudgels if need be.

"How old are you?" I asked.

The girl, Susan Brown, gave me a look for my impudence, and then decided to answer. "Twenty-one." That's how we could always remember her age. She grew up with the century.

Susie was the oldest of fifteen children, born in a whitewashed thatch-roofed cabin close by the shingle in County Clare on the west coast of Ireland. It's still there, still the same, and in 1954 we visited Susie's one remaining brother, the last of the Browns to live there. A cow was munching the sea grass of the low dune as we approached, and just over the hill was the ruin of an old castle.

Susie was the first of the Browns to emigrate. When she came, in 1917, she worked for a time in the New York Telephone Company. What she did for the telephone company we never knew, nor could we imagine, because her schooling had stopped at the third grade, and her brogue, lovely as it was, was a language quite unlikely for a telephone operator. She did on occasion show a throwback to those days, maybe to what she used to hear. When on the telephone she pronounced numbers with the authentic ring of the operator tribe: "Nine-a th-ree, two, th-ree."

"Sure if I'd stayed on in the telephone company I'd not be where I am now," she once said in later days to Kathy, after Kathy had grown up and was a woman herself.

It was true. Susie came to work for us, strangers, and her life became entwined with ours like honeysuckle around young trees. We all grew up together, Harry and I from a young couple into middle age, Tom and Katharine into a man and woman, and Susie into our staff—the best friend that any of us ever had. The one we all turned to in trouble and in happiness.

One by one the other Browns came out from the Old Country. Catherine, the quiet beautiful one, got a job doing housework. Bridie got married young and died in childbirth. Tom got a job on the Madison Avenue streetcars, Davey got a job in the same place, and later they both graduated to Madison Avenue buses. Mary, quiet too, became chambermaid and waitress in a conservative household of wealth, and always bore the manner of the professional. But never Susie. Nor Anna, the youngest to "come out." Anna and Susie were alike, fighting often and loud. There never was a month when all the Browns were speaking to all the others. And the most belligerent, the most deeply emotional, actually the most just, was Susie. But to find justice and exact it, she examined every situation, every conversation, every tone of voice. If there was an implication that besmirched her honor, or that of anyone she held dear, she was a blazing Amazon. Long telephone calls kept the Brown family in constant touch.

Susie did all the work, as was expected of "help" by

every householder of that day. She scrubbed floors on her hands and knees, she did walls on a ladder. She washed the clothes and hung them out on the Riverside Drive roof in bitterest cold. She was a beautiful ironer. Her cooking grew with the years to become the standard by which I still judge all family cooking: the light hot gingerbread; the rich chocolate cake; the lemon chiffon pie with nary a bit of cornstarch, just eggs and lemon and fluff; the big juicy hams; the fabulous mousse; the Thanksgiving turkey with chestnut dressing. The children said that her oatmeal was atrocious. But I said they must eat it and she saw to it that they did.

She did all that was expected of the general houseworker, and far more. She made shoe bags, and bags for dresses before the day when those items could be picked up in the closet shop of a department store. She made chair covers for the summer which we still use, all on her own initiative. She turned cuffs and collars on shirts, and sewed on buttons, frequently not matching. The ring made by her pail of water still remains on a mahogany chest that was my grandmother's. It was handy to leave it there when she was scrubbing down the wall. She left the floor-polisher running, and another round circle, burned into the front-hall floor of the apartment where we still live, will always remind us of her. She was the most untidy person in the world, but at the same time one of the cleanest. Afternoons when she'd had her bath and put on a fresh white Hoover apron, she shone. Her cheeks were red and her forehead polished. She'd walk along the Drive and shout at the children playing. Or go up to Reeves' grocery store to flirt with Phil, the manager, also from the Old Country. She walked with a peasant's gait, the weight of her body shifting from side to side with each step, her arms curved out from her hips. Anyone would turn on the street to watch her swing along in her ripe vitality.

Her social life was as absorbing as our own. Whenever we gave a party she'd get Bridie or Catherine or Mary or Anna to come and help. She'd shout at them and get the work done. We never knew for certain who might appear from the kitchen to pass the food. But we knew it would taste good and it would be served properly, because Mary, the professional, apparently put them all "formal." The only drawback at these parties would be the talk in the kitchen, sometimes louder than at our own table, which wasn't very mild of itself. Our idea of a successful dinner party was general conversation, the whole table joining in. Arguments were lively, sometimes acrimonious, with debaters pounding the table, making the silver jump. Old friends still recall the fervor and the fury and the guest who died of a heart attack a day after one of these sessions.

It was only after our party moved into the living room that the Browns (any number might have gathered by now) would settle down to their meal in the kitchen—on the stove, the sink, the set-tubs. I rarely ventured out. It was better not to know.

One fine big noisy party of ours will always be remembered as "the Russian Party." Our Russian friends from Tula had found friends in the visiting Moscow Art Theater group, the Stanislavsky actors who came over to New York in 1923. (Some of the group did not return to Moscow, among them one from Tula who had been a schoolmate of Sasha. There were also some actors from the "Chauve-Souris" who did not return to Russia, notably the round fat father who sat in front of his tent-like house, strumming his guitar and singing the Russian equivalent of "O Katerina.") They were the occasion for this celebration of ours and for many another—warm-hearted fun-loving people, handing the guitar from one to the other, singing Russian songs through the night, and eating enormously. I remember one man eating seven bananas at a sitting.

That particular Russian evening required extra help,

and Susie and the Browns and their friends had such a party of their own in the kitchen, which opened on the court, that next morning a complaint was registered with the superintendent about the raucous "Irish" party that had gone on all night. The Russian hilarity in the front of the house was apparently wafted out the window over Riverside Drive and the Hudson.

When Susie had a counter-party she always bought the food for it herself: when she entertained it must be her doings. That was her judgment, not mine. In all her days, Susie never wanted to talk money. Once there was an intermission of a year, during which she got married and had a baby. When she came back to work, times had already changed, and I offered her a salary of seventy-five dollars a month. Susie was indignant. "Holy Mother of God, you know I'm not that good!"

She loved and appreciated the presents that we gave her and that our friends gave her over the years, and she always wrote a letter of thanks. There never was a less self-conscious letter-writer than Susie. She was almost illiterate but entirely at ease with pencil and paper. There were no capitals in her letters. Her spelling was strictly phonetic. The only possible way to get the drift was to read the words aloud and not think. Just listen. Then you'd hear Susie's rough voice behind them and her special Clare idiom. I have many of her letters still. They breathe her presence and her good sense.

I suggested that I teach her spelling. We'd do it evenings. "I'm such a dumbbell!" she said. But she wasn't. She was bright and eager and would have caught on in no time. But we never got to it. When she was home taking care of the children, we were out, and whenever we were home, she was out. Susie and I used up every minute of our freedom.

Susie accepted gifts with sincere appreciation. And she gave with her heart—eighteenth-century silver sugar tongs, which she would not have known as eighteenth-century but which by some instinct she knew to be right; fine damask hand towels for Katharine in later years; the best sweater that Tom ever had.

Her social timing was keen. She came to me at a cocktail party when she was passing sandwiches and said under her breath, "There's a lady over there with no one to talk to." Her intelligence was of high order. She could diagnose trouble with a vacuum cleaner or the plumbing, not from experience but from horse sense. She could size up a person or a situation and hit the nail on the head. She passed judgment on all the children's friends and pried into their affairs. She disliked this one and sent him home, she loved that one and let her stay for supper. She kidded loudly and tried to be one of them.

Teddy, a cousin, stayed frequently at our house. He had a girl named Phoebe and it was his contention that Susie read Phoebe's letters. Once he left a pile of Phoebe's letters on his bureau with a note far down in the pile. It said: "Susie, I forbid you to read my letters." After which Susie refused to speak to him for days.

Both the children took music lessons throughout the years she was with us, and it was Susie who saw to it that they got up at seven o'clock to do an hour's practicing before breakfast. When they played at the music school recitals there she was, in the back row, erect and unmoving except for the motion of her jaw. She chewed gum in time to the music.

All Susie's friends knew when Katharine had a beau. When Tom went to the war Susie paid for prayers to be said in her church daily for his safe homecoming. She wrote to him in France and made him a khaki-colored sweater. When he finally came back she knew that it was because of her prayers that had been gloriously answered.

She was a devout Catholic. Once she reminded a Catholic friend of ours that it was an Ember day—just as the friend was helping herself to meat. She made a novena every year and during the nine days of heavy churchgoing wore a purged look and spoke a shade less loud. But in spite of her religion she took on the political cast of the household and was all for the Spanish Loyalists. She went to the voting booth with true Irish fervor, but she asked Harry first to tell her what he thought of the candidates. You could feel her tabulating the pros and cons in her mind as she listened intently, her eyes snapping. She took the newspaper to bed with her at night.—She read every word of *Gone With the Wind*, and went to see *Playboy of the Western World* because it was Irish. But it was far from her idea of Ireland. "Don't be wasting your time," she advised me in disgust.

In later years when Susie's daughter was nearly grown up, she had already moved out of our home but not out of our lives, nor we out of hers. To walk into Susie's flat was to step back fifteen years in our own lives. There was the imitation Chinese blue rug that used to be in our dining room and was now in hers, the familiar curtains, the rose lamp, the pictures of the children. She was still tense, still striving, still pushing too hard. With Michael, her husband, she tried to make a home like the one she had lived in during the best years of her life. But Michael, more recently come from the Old Country than she, and slow of pace, was an irritation, and she was always trying to make Cecilia, her pretty daughter, over into the image of Katharine.

She still came to our house to clean. "How are you, Susie?" Harry would say when he came home from the office and found her still there. "Pretty good for an old lady," she always replied with a short loud laugh.

But she wasn't pretty good. She had worked harder

than any two women all her life. We were a frantic, hurrying family, always trying to do too much, and she took on our ways. Our lives were filled with climaxes, all of which she shared with her whole being. She worked too hard and cared too much. She was a diabetic and had a heart attack. But she kept on smoking in her nervous way and the doctors could not teach her serenity.

She and I used to sit down and talk things over in those days. We both knew that life was no longer the gay perpetual-motion drama-comedy that we had lived together for twenty-eight years. We kissed when we parted. Susie was a sick woman. And I was bowed beneath the sins of my own responsibility, of short-sightedness, of carelessness, that had made me ask too much and let me accept too much.

Susie died in 1950, the day after her fiftieth birthday. She had just gone to bed with the newspaper.

Harry always had breakfast with the children, watch on the table beside his plate—a "Lifetime" Macy watch which I bought him early in our married life and which he still possesses.

I was rarely present at breakfast, but even now my children recall the scene with an eye on me: the oatmeal which Susie put in front of them, and the watch on the table. Harry always has a watch on the table, as it were. Like many intense workers who give so much of themselves to accomplish more than there are hours to accomplish it in, he is obsessed by time. At other people's houses I see him glancing at his wrist (the modern watch, Macy's "Lifetime" notwithstanding); every morning he announces the hour to the household, and sees no reason why everyone he knows should not be ready to answer his telephone call at 8:15.

As I say, I was rarely present at the morning function. From the day my first child was born, up to somewhere in the days of World War II, I might say that I never prepared breakfast, and that a good part of that time I had it served me on a tray. This was not laziness or affluence. But a maid in the house to get breakfast for a growing family was as common those days as not having one is now. We mothers took it for granted. And oh! the peace of that hour between eight and nine! Sabbie, the cat, had jumped over my bed with a trill in his throat and taken up his position on the window sill, the children had finished practicing (in different rooms), had had their breakfast with their dad and kissed me goodbye. Harry had looked over the *Times*. (It was years later before he took the time to read the morning paper through before starting for the office.) And he too had gone. I had read the mail and had a fine busy New York day ahead of me . . .

Anyone who likes cats knows that trill in the throat which is their most intimate greeting, and will recognize how dear to the heart is the memory of one cat particularly beloved. Sabbie was a Maine shag that we got as a kitten on Mount Sabattus near Center Lovell, Maine, in 1925. He was a tiger, and though long-haired, his fur had none of the silky softness one associates with Persians. Maine shags are believed to be the descendants of Persian cats brought over by a sea captain whose ship went aground off the coast of Maine. The cats swam ashore, and this was the result, the coarser fur no doubt due to the cold climate. Sabbie had a magnificent ruff and a powerful body. There is another legend about these cats—that they have mated with raccoons. Which in Sabbie's case seemed not unreasonable. His coloring, gray and white striped with a purely white throat, was raccoon-like, as was his debonair behavior. In one bound he would spring to the mantelpiece or a lady's bare

shoulder or straight up off the ground to catch something
out of your hand. He loved to play hard, and my arms and
hands were torn with scratches.

Sabbie spent as much of the day as we let him on the
window sill of our front bedroom. We were able to keep
him out of our room at night in winter when the doors were
closed. But he was waiting at the threshhold every morning, and the second the door was opened he'd rush in, bound
over me on my bed with that little trill of greeting, and take
up his daily watch. We lived on the ground floor at that
time and were only a little above the level of the street with
an areaway between us and the sidewalk. This, we pre-
sumed, he was guarding. In summer when everything was
wide open Sabbie spent the night on the window sill, and
more than once his dark majestic figure was noted by
friends of ours who chanced to pass. Occasionally he leapt
out and in. And one time he brought in some friends—
three cats were scuffling beneath my bed.

Every June from 1927 on, we moved the entire household out to New Jersey when school was over. Every year
Sabbie was terrified anew. When he got into the cool interior of the New Jersey house, the pupils of his eyes grew
large, his fur stood up and his body flattened nearly to the
floor. He slid underneath the stove or the Hoover cabinet in
the kitchen, and when—much later—he got up courage to
go upstairs, he disappeared under a bed. It took a full
twenty-four hours for him to feel safe in new surroundings.
But once the hurdle was made, he fitted into the life of
woods and fields like the true wild animal that he was.

We never did know what finally happened to Sabbie.
In 1931 when we were all four on a walking trip in Switzerland, dear friends of ours had our house. They wrote us
that Sabbie had disappeared. He could not have been run
over—they had searched the roadway. They called toward

the hill in back of the house. They took their car to other roads and called. When we came back at the end of summer we walked to all the spots he had known well. He used to stroll with us for considerable distances, and now we walked sadly over the same paths, calling "Sabbie, Sabbie!" and listening for that trill we loved so much. But Sabbie never came back. Perhaps he reverted. There are raccoons in our woods.

Khaki was a jaunty Airedale female who wandered up Hardscrabble, our road, stopped at our house and stayed for the rest of her life. We notified the police and advertised in the local paper, but no one claimed her. She was well bred, handsome on the rare occasions when we had her plucked and her legs weren't coated with mud or her curly fur stuck full of burrs. And her manners were perfection until she'd spent her first summer in our careless household and learned how easy it was to get round us.

Khaki enjoyed life more and got more out of it than any creature, man or animal, that I have ever known. She was a wanderer, but she always came back. Sometimes she was gone overnight, once for a week, and when she got back the pads of her paws were raw. Her very good pal was a heavy black police dog named (I'm sorry to say) Nigger. Nigger by instinct was a watchdog. He would have preferred to stay in front of the Stimsons' house where he lived to protect his own people. But Khaki lured him on. People used to report the pair far, far away. Once big lumbering Nigger was hit by a car up on the main road from Bernardsville to Mendham about three miles from Hardscrabble. He was found there, prostrate, with a blond Airedale standing over him, growling until someone she knew came to the rescue. We were in frequent communication with the police about Khaki—which was not easy, since we had no telephone. They would send us word from time to time that our dog was seen here—or there—to forestall a call from us.

Khaki also went back and forth with us between city and country, usually in the back seat with the guests. She was not a good traveler and frequently was carsick. Friends who knew her well could warn us in time to stop to let her out. But sometimes we were too late. Back in New York we had her mated to a thoroughbred. This was to give the children a practical lesson in the facts of life, and we chose the thoroughbred as a salute to what we considered her own good breeding. Unfortunately for education the children had already gone to bed when the labor pains started, and were fast asleep by the time the first puppy was born. When the last of nine slipped out, it was four in the morning. Harry and I were dead tired, and utterly inadequate, but Khaki knew just what to do and did it, and the next morning at breakfast we had a basket filled with little damp black creatures to show our children.

The puppies were born in the kitchen, but Susie could not have them under her feet, so we transferred them to a hall closet, which so conditioned them that when they had been weaned and given away, the report was that they all sought out dark closets in their new homes.

Grown Airedales are handsome. But Airedale puppies are unbelievably no-count, slimy-black and featureless. One day when Katharine was having her cello lesson in the living room, with her teacher sitting opposite facing down the room, and nodding his head to the rhythm of her piece, she saw his eyes suddenly begin to bulge. He was a reserved Englishman, not given to jokes or easy humor. What he saw, crawling along the green carpet, was a line of very small black creatures, nose to tail, moving slowly as one across the room. Like a long black snake.

When these same puppies—minus two, which we had given away—were about three months old, we went again on one of our family walking trips, leaving the household in Bernardsville this time to another friend. The puppies had their own runway with a trough for food and big basin for water. It wouldn't have been too much to ask of our friends as guardian, if Khaki had behaved herself. But endearing as she was, Khaki was not a good mother, and one night she managed somehow to get the puppies out of their runway and led them quietly away. "Get lost!" was her idea. In the morning she was home wagging her tail, infinitely relieved, and ready for breakfast. But the runway was empty. Our poor friend, with all these wellborn creatures in her custody, was frantic. She drove, called, tramped, and finally rounded them up in a field, scattered but all eventually accounted for—on the old country road to Morristown, a route we seldom used, about a mile and three-quarters from home.

We have had other dogs and other cats. We have had other helpers in our home. But that time and those personalities seem so beautiful in retrospect as to be almost legendary. It hardly seems possible that life could have been so completely satisfying.

X

THE THIRTIES

Of all the New York decades that I am now looking back on, the period of the thirties has left the least attractive flavor—and not because of the Depression.

The Depression was indeed Jove's thunderbolt. The stock market crashed. Riches shriveled. Building came to a standstill. In the twenties, as now in the sixties, new apartment houses, banks, office buildings, kept shooting up —pushing their fine heads skyward with the attendant mess in the streets at their feet. "I don't want to come back to New York till it's finished," said a visitor. Now—in 1930— it was finished, not to be touched for a period of twenty years. Frivolity gave way to earnestness. Jimmy Walker no longer dancing at the Casino, entertaining queens, was followed by the incorruptible La Guardia who loved his city with a fiercely burning passion.

By the middle thirties, 16,000,000 across the country were unemployed; 5,000,000 were on relief. From Riverside Drive we looked down on a village of shanties on the edge of the Hudson, huts made of pieces of board picked up in dumps, with gasoline tins cut open and flattened out for roofs, and an old pipe for a chimney. Many of the huts had a small garden with a few potatoes, tomatoes, beans. Hobo jungles grew up around every big city. On our Friday afternoon trips out to New Jersey we saw the patchwork of tiny gardens in the Meadows stretching out for miles, and in each garden a man digging, silhouetted against the sunset. Hundreds of thousands of people roamed the roads. Shabby men sold apples on street corners. Breadlines formed.

Some of it was not so grim. The smoke curling up out of those crooked little chimneys along the Hudson looked cozy to us, and the man on the doorstep in the morning, with his mug of coffee, was an individual who was not going to be downed. The vegetables grown on the Jersey Meadows, nurtured as they were by city refuse, were bigger and better than any we grew. The old men in Central Park still played checkers in the drafty old summer house—in those days we walked through the Park in safety—even though their board was drawn in chalk on a wooden picnic table, and their checkers were beer-bottle tops. But much more important was the exhilarating effect that hard times had on many women. Men lost their jobs, but not all lost their homes, and this was where the woman of the house for the first time really came into her own. She was vital to the new economy. She could scrape and was glad to do it. Every cent counted, and the woman somehow understood better than her husband how to deal with this penny-saving. Some women got jobs where the men could not get them, and this too produced a new self-reliance which has never receded. (Now every third worker in the country is a woman.) What the effects may have been on the children of those Depression households, today's men and women in their forties can say best. Certainly they heard constant talk about money and the lack of it.

Politically the thirties were shot through with fear and hate: The injustice of the Spanish Civil War stirred the souls of the fair-minded. A government had won by honest vote of the people only to have to defend itself by fighting its own citizenry—a government isolated, unaided by the democratic countries from whom it could well have expected to find aid, including Great Britain and the United States; fighting a losing battle against the men and arms sent by Germany and Italy, who in turn were trying out their weapons for a greater war to follow.

In the early days we espoused the Loyalist cause with our whole hearts, as did nearly everyone we knew. We met and talked with people fresh from Madrid, American reporters and Spanish government officials. We went down to the Catalan restaurant on Cherry Street under the arch of Brooklyn Bridge, and sat in the kitchen where three-hundred-pound El Padrone cooked us *arroz con pollo*. We learned to drink wine the Spanish way, from long-spouted leather bottles held on the shoulder. We gave a reception for Isabella Valencia, here to plead her country's cause, and nearly lost our apartment for being "Reds." We helped buy ambulances. To our way of thinking it was a clear-cut issue —before Russia's entry and the subsequent confusion.

The evils of Hitler mounted and horrified the world. Mussolini was bombing helpless Ethiopian villages. And the discrepancies in our own country made us ashamed: Huey Long running his state like a racketeer, Father Coughlin preaching hate over the air, the Red Witch Hunt beginning.

The trend of events inclined thinking people toward the Left.

With the election of Franklin Roosevelt and the beginning of the New Deal, the political radicals and the academic liberals, who had been more or less submerged in garrets or universities during the brash years that followed the Great War, now blossomed forth. Many were called to Washington, and their self-confidence, which for a long time had been lacking, was restored.

It was the day of the intellectual snob. People didn't question. They asserted. There was a word for everything: British imperialism, economic royalists, the Forgotten Man, Bourbons. Everything was black and white. There was no gray. If the other feller didn't have the answer on the tip of his tongue, he was wrong. Communists, fellow travelers, dissenters, disaffected liberals, met on common ground in the Popular Front, and anyone who breathed disagreement was dismissed as a Fascist. It was the Age of Arrogance— a grim time for the patient searcher for truth.

Books and music and travel loomed large with us during those years, perhaps as an escape.

As far back as 1914 we had been Philharmonic subscribers (and still are). For twenty years we sat in aisle seats in the fourth row of the top balcony of Carnegie Hall, pushing breathlessly up those steep stairs immediately after dinner every other Thursday. I marvel that we didn't have strokes—but we were still young. We went through the thin years of Josef Stransky's conducting, the years of the war when one by one the Germans of the orchestra disappeared to return to the Vaterland; through Bodanzky, when the New York Symphony combined with the Philharmonic; Mengelberg from Amsterdam; Furtwängler from Berlin. We were still there when Toscanini took over as permanent conductor, and at that point—the better to do him honor—we moved down to the dress circle. But alas, we heard less well, and we sorely missed the friendly com-

panions with whom we'd been surrounded up top. In front
of us, now in the dress circle, sat Mr. and Mrs. La Guardia,
the mayor with his coat always open, wearing no vest, hair
untidy. Whenever I complained to my husband of his own
lack of sartorial fastidiousness, he argued that if it was all
right for the Little Flower, it was all right for him. How La
Guardia loved that music! How blessed we all were who sat
through those glorious years when the Maestro hurried on
to the podium, giving only a skimpy nod to the audience,
the quicker to bring forth the heavenly music that only he
could create. The sounds of the orchestra under Toscanini,
particularly in Beethoven, are etched in my brain. I find
myself still able to compare them with the renditions that
now come our way—his fast tempo, precise phrasing, the
sweetness of the fiddles. It is a phase of memory that I am
deeply thankful for—that I am constantly fearful may fade
away.

But the world of music really opened up to us as our
children shaped into musicians. Their musical education
took on us as much as on them, until eventually concerts
superseded the theater in our extracurricular life.

The full effect of music on their lives is something I
cannot even now fully assess. And I shall not try. But their
eagerness in the young years was one of the high points of
my own life. Their understanding and appreciation was
genuine and selfless. For them the shining world lay ahead.
Yet even then their very innocence saddened me a little,
knowing as I did only too well what life does to destroy the
clear white directness of youth.

Nature had endowed them with the ear and sense of
rhythm so essential for musical development, and we saw
to it that they had every opportunity—lessons in reading
music notes when they were very young, lest they play too
easily by ear; and concerts, but not too many, so that they

would not be surfeited. Then, with that compulsion on my part never to miss anything, never to let my family miss anything, which has pushed us all into an overloaded existence, I took them to opera. I myself had heard very little opera, and dismissed what I had heard.

In the high-handed way of the uninformed I would have said that I actively disliked Wagner. But I took the children to the *Ring* as a part of their education. In those days it was sung on four afternoons in spring, and before each performance we went to hear Walter Damrosch discourse on the leitmotifs. His exuberance as he played them and sang them was catching. It was a musical experience which the children took in their stride, but which for me was a revelation. It hallowed the "Nibelungenlied" story forever in my memory, and when I hear it now—the war cries of the Valkyries, the forest murmurs, the powerful inevitable descending scale of Wotan's Law—I am transported to that lost Valhalla of so long ago, when I used to sit in the dark opera house between two eager children, the gold curtain still closed, waiting for the opening strains of the river Rhine, and the swaying Rhine Maidens.

In 1934, the four of us were in Europe. We were on a Finnish ship sailing from Hull to Helsinki, when, crossing the cold stormy North Sea, we heard the solemn intonations of the funeral march from *Götterdämmerung* coming out of the low-lying clouds. It was coming from Vienna by radio, from the funeral of Dollfuss, Chancellor of Austria, who had been assassinated.

Tom has never swerved by a grace note from the straight path on which he started out at the age of four. Music has been his life, interrupted only on the surface by five years in the Army, where, he said, his top sergeant reminded him of no one so much as his piano teacher, Isabella

Vengerova: formidable demands and unquestioning obedi-
ence. Underneath, the current apparently continued to run
strong. After the war he became, in time, a conductor with
his own orchestra, and in the city that has probably the
richest musical fare in the world he has carved out a unique
niche. His symphonic programs have brought forth works
quite unknown to present-day audiences, and his operas in
concert form have caught and held the public ear. Most of
them have been in the standard repertoire in Europe, but
never given in New York—or not for a long, long time—so
that the eager musical audience over here is deeply grateful.
To do this has taken not only initiative but a great deal of
courage.

The opening night of these new opera-concerts was a
momentous occasion for him—for all of us. The program
consisted of two one-act operas, a Monteverdi and a Stravinsky. The performance was scheduled to start at eight
o'clock. But that day the Cuba-Russia missile-base deal was
disclosed, and the whole country was in a state of alarm.
President Kennedy let it be known in the afternoon that he
was going to address the American people at seven o'clock.
And so he did. We were all tied to our TV sets, because
might this not be the prelude to another Pearl Harbor? Yet
there wasn't a vacant seat at the concert. The Monteverdi
got going at eight-thirty, only a half-hour late, and the good
music soothed our frantic spirits . . . In the 1963-64 season the opening concert was scheduled for November 25—
the day when all the world mourned.

On that Finnish boat to Helsinki in 1934 we were actually on our way to Russia. It was a period of lull—after the
famine and before the purges—the short space of time when
American tourists were warmly welcomed. Many American

engineers were over there in technical positions, and in our three weeks' stay in Moscow our children met several of their children. (I suppose the meetings came about through Intourist, who had us constantly in hand.) With their new friends our two went dancing. And dancing in Russia at that time meant a thousand or more people gathered in the enormous spaces of the Park of Joy and Culture, pacing through the steps of square dances to the loud strains of amplified orchestra music. Everything in Moscow was amplified. But that scene in the park on a warm summer night was exciting beyond belief, especially to our children.

Their young American friends over there were living much like the Russian children, not quite so crowded perhaps, but with their time apportioned the same between school and work. To Tom and Katharine, who at home went to school in an ordinary way, the Russian combination of lessons and work was to be envied. At seven in the morning these others were on their lathes or looms or what-not, getting paid for it, and evenings they were dancing in the park. For holidays there were trips to the workers' hotels in the Crimea, usually without parents. Gladly would our two have signed up and stayed on.

From Moscow we went down south on a walking trip. Most of our vacations, whether in twos or fours, have been planned around walking trips. But this one in Russia was a fluke. Morris Hindus, American spokesman for Russia in the very earliest days, was in Moscow when we were, and offered to take us on a trip to a collective farm. He had a notion about taking us east of Moscow to the region where he had lived as a boy. But Intourist saw it otherwise and headed us south. They got us tickets for Naltchik, a provincial town north of the Caucasus and south of the river Don, and we meekly proceeded according to their pleasure. Though I do not think they designed it as such, that long

three-day trip of itself gave us a far better idea of Russia
than any trip we could have made to a collective farm.
Every morning when we looked out it was the same as the
day before: like Kansas—level—endless. Sometimes fields
of cabbage stretched as far as the eye could see, guarded by
men with guns. In the distance a village was marked by an
onion-shaped steeple.

The train was long and overflowing with families on
the move, children, food, blankets, bags. At every stop
someone of the family hustled out with kettle in hand to get
hot water for *tchai* (tea). A spigot out of which ran boiling
water, easily accessible to train travelers, was regulation
equipment of every railroad station—a wonderful custom
that all other countries might well copy. In our first-class
car we had a samovar in constant use, and excellent *tchai*
always ready, served in a long glass with a spoonful of jam.
For breakfast there was caviar in individual bowls, like oatmeal. Otherwise the food was without distinction. The head
waiter was a tense civil servant. Late at night we would find
him alone in the diner, adding, tallying. He had to make
five copies of the checks for everything that we ate at each
of our four meals a day, with prices. Not only *our* meals,
but those of all his first-class passengers as well. A country
of bookkeepers, indeed.

One of the passengers whom we got to know was a
Russian chemist. He was struggling with English and
eager to try it out on us. Where were we going, he asked,
and when we told him "Naltchik," he raised his shoulders.
"Why Naltchik?" he asked. We began to wonder too. *All
the way over from America and going to Naltchik!* Maurice
Hindus didn't know why we were going. He'd never been
there. And our friend's continued deprecatory shrugs suggested that we would find Naltchik about as interesting as
Jersey City.

His English vocabulary contained fewer than twenty words, I'd say, but, supplemented with pencil drawings and gestures and a worn map, he told us about a fabulous country not too far from Naltchik but deep in the mountains, where men still wore armor and lived in stone castles built by the Crusaders. The country was Svanetia.

It does not seem possible now, but we did it. We left Maurice Hindus to visit the collective farms listed by Intourist, while we escaped and entrained on a trip into the past. Nobody had ever asked Intourist about Svanetia. Intourist, in Naltchik, turned out to be a single person who was also the only one in town who could speak English. Her name was Sonia, she was eighteen years old, and she went with us into Svanetia.

We were six people. Besides the four of us English-speaking Americans and Sonia, English- and Russian-speaking, there was Samat, our Moslem guide who spoke Russian and Svan, the language of the country which we were about to penetrate. Samat, complete with horse to carry provisions, came from the Balkarian Republic, then one of the integral states of the Soviet, but since that time liquidated. (We never saw Samat once without his turban, though we were all to sleep together on the ground and in the hay, and at sunrise and sunset, regardless of weather, he slipped away to face Mecca and say his prayers.)

Svanetia can be entered only two months of the year because of the surrounding mountains, through which the lowest pass, covered by a glacier, is ten thousand feet. That is the pass from the north over which we were to climb.

For this undertaking we "outfitted" ourselves at a little chalet in a pine forest eighty-five miles south of Naltchik. It was a charming spot and, except for bedbugs, might have been in Switzerland. But it was no Abercrombie & Fitch. As we stood, we were entirely unequipped. Our clothes were for country-walking only—low shoes, wool skirts, wool pants, unlined jackets. And our food, provided by mine host of the chalet, got out of hand somewhere in the process of the three-language hurdle. Our only definite request was for hard-boiled eggs, three dozens of them. Other than that, we felt it best to accept what the country had to offer. We never saw the food until we reached the edge of the glacier, where we had our first meal. But there it was: an enormous round cheese, several loaves of coarse bread, enough *tchai*, a bag of sugar, butter, and a huge bag heavy with greasy salami-type pork sausages. Samat, good Moslem, could not eat the pork, he would not even allow it in the same saddlebag with the food which he did plan to eat, so we had to repack it, and never again on the trip was it taken out. We weren't Moslems, but we could not face that sausage. The package containing what we thought was to be the three dozen eggs turned out to be three dozen boxes of Pushkin crackers. Whether it was an error in translation or a shortage of supply we never knew. The crackers were Soviet-made, of ersatz material, faintly and unpleasantly sweetish, limp and crumbly. The coarse bread was good. The cheese was good. The *tchai* was nectar. It would have been enough except that we had to let Samat have most of the bread on account of his pork complex. And then the butter. On the first day, on our way up the glacier, Samat's horse slipped and cut herself. It was a slight cut, but Samat, to whom his horse meant infinitely more than assorted foreigners and Intourist, put butter on her wound and continued throughout the trip to administer the same treatment, with the result that none of us ever ate an ounce of butter after that first luncheon at the edge of the glacier. What we actually subsisted on was Pushkin crackers and cheese with *tchai* to wash it down. Once in Svanetia we found fresh raspberries, and a Svan farmer gave us cold boiled potatoes, without exception the finest-tasting food I ever remember. Gourmet food.

Climbing the glacier was hard, but descending the other side was worse because it was longer. "Down, always down," moaned Sonia, fresh from the School of Culture. We went down practically to sea level. The rocks through which we zigzagged were jagged. The horse took infinite care and so did we. It was after sunset when we reached our encampment for the night in a hardwood forest. It was the Svan equivalent of an alpine hut, two tents without floors or furniture, an open fire for cooking, boxes on which to sit, and a smiling Svan couple to greet us. Besides our party of six and the Svans, there were two others, a Russian father and son who had just descended from Mount Elbruz and were on their way out. They arrived immediately after us.

That night in the Svan camp was one in a lifetime. Tired as we were, the meal around the open fire must have restored us for we sat on and on until long after midnight, engaged in the most incongruous conversation on record. We didn't discuss politics or nations, but under the tall trees, in the shadow of the highest mountain in Europe, we all had our say—the children as well as the others—on what we wanted of life, and what we could give—our individual, spiritual aspirations and evaluations. The translating was quick and unhesitant. Looking back, it was imperceptible. The firelight played on Samat's turban, on the Svans' long Italian-type noses and soft brown eyes, the round-faced light-haired tall Russians, Sonia's adolescent eagerness.

Svanetia was paradise. In fact, maybe the original paradise. What with its extraordinary natural beauty and the fact that it is near enough to the Holy Land possibly to have been known, there has been serious surmise that this may have been the biblical Garden of Eden. The melting snow from the mountains keeps it fresh, and the sun, of

African hotness, brings forth blossoms of great size and in
rich abundance. We walked knee-deep in yellow lilies. The
wild rhododendron bushes, which must be a blaze of strong
color in spring, were like trees. Even the most common
flowers were giant-size and deeply toned—clover, butter-
cups, daisies . . .

It is a tiny country, reputedly with twenty-six thousand inhabitants, though how anyone would know I don't
see. There isn't a wheel and scarcely a road in its entire extent. We had been told that the Svans did not relish visitors. But a farmer, whose name had been given Samat and
Sonia, received us hospitably, and let us camp in his barn
for three nights. Apparently he was well known and respected. Word of our arrival must have got round, because
from time to time a horseman would dash into the barnyard
and pull up short. None looked friendly, but they abided by
our host. I doubt if any Svans we saw knew that the Czar
was gone. Somebody still collected taxes, and as such was
an enemy. But inevitable.

One afternoon when the sun was too hot for field
work, the farmer's sons and daughter sat in the barn door-
way and sang—maybe for us, maybe for themselves. The
instrument they strummed was a homemade guitar-of-sorts.
When a string broke the girl ran out to a horse in the yard
and pulled a hair out of his tail to replace it. The songs
seemed to come from a faraway ancient day, and as they
played and sang, an airplane flew over us high in the sky.
It came from a world we had already almost forgotten, and
I, for one, at that moment wanted never to leave. Civilization had nothing to offer.

But leave we did, at 3 A.M. in the dark, from the same
Svan camp in the forest, up ten thousand feet and then
down, arriving exhausted eighteen hours later, again in
darkness, at the chalet from which we started.

We didn't know which we wanted more, a hot bath or

a good meal. Actually, we got neither. There was no hot water, and the bus which was to bring in food from Nalt-chik had not arrived. What we were offered for dinner that night was the greasy sausages which we couldn't force our-selves to eat on our trip, and which had stayed untouched in the left-hand saddlebag.

Maurice Hindus was waiting for us, and here we also met the biology son of H. G. Wells. He was going into Svanetia the next day and had provided himself with several flat bottles of vodka, one of which he invited us to share there and then. He was the third Britisher on record to en-ter Svanetia, and we were the fifth, sixth, seventh and eighth Americans. (Julian Bryan with a photographer and two other companions had made it earlier.)

We were disenchanted with Russia in spite of the fun we had and the enthusiasm of our teen-age children. In Moscow we had a long intimate talk with a young woman —wife, mother, doctor's helper. She was a relative of one of our Russian friends in New York and came to see us in our hotel bedroom in Moscow. She could speak no English, but brought with her a faded elderly lady wearing an ankle-long skirt of rusty black, and carrying a large umbrella, the very caricature of an old-fashioned German governess. She had been a lady-in-waiting on the Czarina and was the daughter of a famous general. The Soviet tolerated her be-cause of her age but gave her no ration card, and she sub-sisted on what she could get by translating. Like so many leftovers from the old regimes of Europe, this old lady was confident that the White Russians, with all the western world behind them, were assembling outside the walls of Russia to free them.

The young woman was not so naïve. She told us in great detail about the Soviet way of life, the enthusiasm demanded for parades, the disillusion of the nurses and doctors of the hospital staff where she worked, above all the danger of speaking freely before her little boy. Before they talked to us at all, the two looked out the windows and drew the curtains. They did not use the elevator up or down.

We met another relative openly, a man who was a professor at the university. He said nothing against the regime, but how he ate! And how he longed to go to America!

This was fourteen years after Lincoln Steffens had seen the future, and Jack Reed had died for it. What we saw were people afraid—as the next few years of the purges showed they had reason to be.

Someone once said that we were a family that enjoyed discomfort, and our travel choices would seem to confirm this. When the four of us went together the procedure was to walk with a pack on the back, but to sleep indoors whenever possible. We did the Presidential Range in New Hampshire, sleeping in the huts, at an age when two of us should have known better. On the first day out, climbing the steep trail of Lafayette, Harry gave up completely and lay down flat on the trail. "I'm like the Ford—all right on the downhill." And on the last day when we finally descended Mount Madison and dragged through endless fields toward the nearest hotel, my ankles were swollen to three times their size. "That," the doctor announced when we saw him days later, "is what is known in the army as 'footsore.' "

Undaunted, we tried the Green Mountain Trail the next year, coming off the mountains each night to sleep in a farmhouse, which turned out to be far more difficult than staying in the huts, however uncomfortable. We plodded through streams, the rain drenched us, our leather coats were one time so water-soaked that though Mrs. Bean, our landlady of the night, hung them behind the kitchen stove, they were still steaming the next morning.

In later years, when the children had outgrown us, we

still walked and still enjoyed discomfort. The list is long of Gasthofs in the Tyrol, broken-down manor houses in Carinthia, and inns in out-of-the-way Swiss valleys. Travel for both of us has been like reading, each trip a book, fascinating, but not really part of ourselves—not since those bouts in the thirties with the children.

Our travels with the children bore fruit. Not many years ago, Katharine, moved away from music now and into writing, spent six weeks with Axel, her husband, and a small band of intrepid scientists, eight in all, on Bylot Island in eastern Canada, north of Baffin Bay, and four hundred and fifty miles north of the Arctic Circle. They were watching the bird cycle (among other natural phenomena): the arrival of the birds from the south, the mating, nesting, appearance of baby birds and preparations for migration south—all telescoped into a few weeks of twenty-four-hour-long days. This was only one study of many on that famous trip—the phenomena of frost action, the weather, the physiology of the Eskimos, the interdependence of plant and insect life in that brief span of spring. Out of this Katharine wrote *Spring on an Arctic Island*, an evocation of that pale beige world, flat, horizonless, a monotone broken only by a dark spot of water when the ice finally began to melt, by the figure of a hooded Eskimo, by the swift-moving sled pulled by eight dark Huskies . . . They let the long slow northern peace enter their hearts. They lived for a while in the springtime of mankind.

XI

THE RETREAT

Nowadays automobiles are not newsworthy. People are as casual about them as about refrigerators. But in our life cars have been sensational.

In 1927, when things were on the up and up and our children were at the age to need an anchorage in the country for long school vacations, we bought the house in New Jersey. And for that reason we were obliged also to buy a car.

But first about the house. It was October when we turned into Hardscrabble Road, Bernardsville, and found ourselves on a pathway of gold, maples brilliant over our heads, and the road carpeted with the yellow leaves of tulip trees. The road ran beside a strong-flowing stream, and in a mile and a half we passed only two houses and two abandoned mills. At the third house we stopped. It was a small pre-Revolutionary field-stone house with two immensely tall spruce trees in front, two barns—one ramshackle, the other usable—and five and a half acres, mostly woodland. During the Revolution it had been used as a commissariat, we learned, and on the hill behind it the New Jersey brigade had encamped during the bitter cold winter of 1779-80. Now it was quiet and gray, with walls twenty-four inches thick.

We bought it within a day—for four thousand dollars. It is a magical figure for us. Harry started his business life on that amount and the house in Bernardsville gave us a refuge for the rest of our lives.

Only thirty-five miles from New York, it is really a forgotten valley. Deer are so plentiful that we hear them on winter nights chewing the ivy leaves off our walls. Muskrats have a mound on the edge of the pond opposite the house. Raccoons eat our corn. A pileated woodpecker flaps over the treetops, back and forth, all through the cool and cold months. Wood ducks visit us in spring, Canada geese in fall. We might as well be in the Adirondacks. And although it is so close to New York, it is a hard spot to locate. When we moved in, in 1928, we ordered furniture from Macy's, and camped in the house awaiting it. Late of a Saturday afternoon a huge Macy's truck drove up. (In those days Macy's did its own trucking.) The driver was out of his mind. "How did *you* find Macy's?" he shouted at us.

We had no telephone, no furnace and no electricity for twelve years, and the absence of all these so-called conveniences constituted a blessing that very few people appreciate. Doing without a telephone kept away city trippers looking for a Sunday visit in the country; we had three good fireplaces and a big kitchen range—the most deliciously comforting all-purpose form of heat I have ever known. Our

reading lamps were big shiny metal affairs with opaque
white glass shades that gave off a soft glow. We had plenty
of them, one beside each bed. And in the kitchen were lamps
on wall brackets with reflectors. We had an iceman.

For the luxury of this privacy, however, it was neces-
sary to have an automobile. We had in the past owned a
car. Our first was a 1917 Model T which we had to crank
each morning to get started. This was during a summer on
Long Island, and each morning Harry was convinced—
often rightly—that he would miss the train. We were living out in Brookhaven, innocent then of atom bomb and
laboratories, and a good two-hour train trip from the city.
When the car acted up I tried to get him to Patchogue by
a short cut where we sometimes caught up with the train,
or, missing that, to Babylon where he caught one on another line. This was regulation for the Ford.

The Maxwell, our second car, was probably the worst
car ever made. It fell to pieces—literally—on a Canadian
trip which Molly and I took together. We had driven up
through Maine and the back roads of Quebec, which were
enough to shake any car, but shattered the Maxwell. On
our return the gas tank fell off—to the ground—and had
to be fastened back with wire by a French Canadian *mé-
canicien*. In New York State, as night was falling, the brake
gave out on a hill near Fishkill, and we had to depend on
the emergency for the rest of the way home, which was one
long hill down.

But our real drama began with the Lincoln. It was a
touring car, open to the elements. We bought it in 1927,
second-hand, third-hand, fourth-hand—who knows. And we
drove it steadily for ten years. Summer and winter the back
seat was filled with children, dogs, friends. The parent-
hosts sat smugly in front while the others, during the bitter
months, huddled together in blankets in the rear. We knew

nothing of the mechanicism of a car and did nothing for the faithful old Lincoln in those ten years except fill it up with gas, change tires—often—and have the fenders straightened after mishaps. The top got so shabby that we couldn't put it up on a windy day. And an electrical difficulty developed which no one ever properly diagnosed. It sometimes stopped us dead for as long as an hour. The big car loaded with people and animals always attracted a crowd, and usually in those early days of cars there'd be a mechanical wiseacre among them who itched to get his hands into a Lincoln engine. I remember one such in Kearney, New Jersey, and another in Jersey City. Those were the days of no Pulaski Skyway, no turnpike, not even a tunnel under the Hudson. We had to follow the streetcars from Newark to Hoboken, there to wait in line for the ferry, children tired after a full weekend, and we ourselves in an agony of fear that the car would again stop dead.

In the beginning, when we were still getting Bernardsville settled, a little at a time, I was the driver. Harry had got rusty in the years since the Maxwell, and was too busy to learn over again. Not until we moved out for the first summer did he begin to take over, but he didn't wait quite long enough. One summer evening after an early supper we started out for South Orange to play bridge. Every detail stands out. It was a lovely evening, the top was down, and I was feeling fine in a new lavender linen dress. But on the last curve of Hardscrabble, Harry made too wide an arc. The big car slid off the road and slowly descended a steep bank. Instead of turning over as any other car would do, it kept upright, and when it reached the bottom just leaned heavily against an apple tree.

We had to find a house with a telephone, give up our bridge game, and walk home. "This was so unnecessary," was my unkind remark which for some reason has come down in the annals.

No one was hurt, but the left running board and fender were a shambles, which was unfortunate on many counts but particularly because the next day Harry had to go to Somerville, the county seat, to take his driver's test. He did go; and he took the test in the crumpled Lincoln. How they could have let that pass I don't know. But he got his license and never lost it. Nor has he had another accident.

The end of the Lincoln is shrouded in mystery. In later days we gave up the Sunday night returns. We'd send the children in by train to Susie and to school, and we would go back Monday morning. One Monday the Lincoln had a flat. A neighbor's boy passing by on his way to work offered to help. He put on the spare, but with misgivings. It was in such condition, said he, that we'd never reach New York. However, we had little choice. We loaded her up as we always did, with produce, typewriter, suitcases, and then went to Morristown—warily—so that Harry at least could get to the city. He took the train and I started on my slow fearful journey alone. By that time the Holland Tunnel was in operation, and I had the temerity to drive through it, promising myself with every turn of the wheels that once I reached the garage I would never again set foot in that car.

But I didn't reach the garage. On West End Avenue and Seventy-fourth Street, right behind the mansion of Charles Schwab, I heard a sickening sizzle and knew that the tire had breathed its last. I got to the curb, telephoned from the nearest apartment house to the garage about my trouble and my location, and then transferred the luggage to a taxi and went on home to Riverside Drive. For once I was really shaken. I telephoned Harry, who was already immersed in his own problems, mine entirely forgotten, and made the announcement that *never again* . . .

By Thursday I got his attention sufficiently to make a date to look for a new car. We'd see what, if anything, we could get for the Lincoln; and for its best possible appearance we'd have it washed and the torn top put down. In those days we kept the car in a garage on Little Broadway just north of 125th Street. It was run by Ecuadorians, and a more faithful gentlemanly crew of service men I have never seen. They would come at any hour to pick up the car, or deliver it. Nothing was too much trouble. So I now telephoned the Ecuadorians and asked them to proceed. "But where is the car?" asked Raoul, the head man.

Helpful as always, they had gone down to Seventy-fourth Street and West End Avenue when I telephoned, put on a tire which they had brought along, and left the car. Madame, they assumed, was in the apartment house from which she had telephoned, waiting to pick up the car when finished. Though it was now three days later, Harry and I went down to West End where all we found was an empty spot. That was the end of an era. (A few years later we thought we saw the Lincoln in Haiti.)

Bernardsville has changed a little but not much through the years. In due course we added two more rooms and put in a furnace and electricity. Our only concession to an earlier way of life is that our telephone number is unlisted. We have eleven beds, and during our children's college years every bed was filled every weekend. Walks around the pond by moonlight, games in the barn, tennis and croquet were our pleasure. Poison ivy, snakes, black flies and wasps were our handicaps. We never suffered much from mosquitoes, and field mice we rather enjoyed. Certainly our cat enjoyed them. Besides him there was always a dog—a series of dogs that started with dear, dear Khaki, and went on through Woolly, her son; Dugan, a long-lived golden retriever; and Blitz, a handsome police dog whose uncontrollable excitement brought him to an early end. He used to try to bite the tires off the front wheels of passing cars. All the dogs were wanderers with a wide territory to roam in, and through the years there was always the sound of Harry's voice as darkness fell, in front of the house, behind the house, calling Dugie, Blitzie, Woolly—calling, calling—for them to come home.

It is very quiet in Bernardsville now. A few houses have been built along Hardscrabble which makes it more cheery when we drive out on Friday night. "The Buckleys are still up." "The Moodys must have company." We have a Labrador retriever, female, who always steps aside into the ditch when a car approaches, and prefers our company and our home to the Wild Beyond. We now drive a Volkswagen.

XII

BOOKS

In the early days of our marriage—in those days of annual moving—bookshelf space was no problem. Now after fifty years the wall of our living room stretches from floor to ceiling in a tapestry of multicolored volumes. It indicates the course our lives have taken, as well as the changing taste of our literary appetites.

Sometimes in a tired moment I sit on the sofa across the room and let my eye roam over the shelves. It is an esthetic pleasure for one thing—that high broad patterned wall. Here and there I spot a book whose very cover warms my heart. But more often I am oppressed by those shiny new volumes that still have to be read.

On the top shelf, reachable only by ladder, are the few treasures that we both brought from our premarital existence and that nothing shall wrest from us: *The Conquest of Mexico* and *The Conquest of Peru; Anna Karenina* and *The Mill on the Floss;* Henty, Barrie—all redolent of enchantment. Stacked up there almost too far away to identify, they are the shabby but dignified survivors of uncomplicated days when a book was just for pleasure.

Though we did not own many books in those earliest days, we read voraciously, supplying ourselves from the nearby public library. Never throughout the years has reading meant so much to me as when I wheeled one baby out in the afternoon, then two babies, with a library book tucked under the blanket. Like most New York mothers I felt impelled to get my children into the fresh air of park or campus or riverside—as early as possible, and for as long as possible. "Neither snow, nor rain, nor heat . . ." deterred us. Unlike their suburban cousins, our children could not be wheeled in just because it was too cold or too hot. In New York, at least in those days, babies stayed out their allotted time. And mothers with them.

I read every Joseph Conrad on the library shelves, every Balzac that the library saw fit to carry, and every Henry James. It was a trio hard to beat and became the foundation of literary comparison for the rest of my life. Conrad up to then had been "far out." A snobbish little Conrad club, encouraged, if I remember right, by Christopher Morley, considered him their own. But in 1914, or thereabout, Doubleday, Page & Co. tried selling a set of Conrad by mail. It was one of the first ventures of its kind, and the man who wrote the ads was none other than my young com panion-at-arms.

The Mercantile Library, at that time down on Astor Place, was a boon. It was founded (in 1820, I recently learned) "to discourge young merchants' clerks from spending their evenings lounging on street corners or frequenting questionable places of amusement." You could get everything there and never needed to wait. Friday afternoons I'd go down by subway with an armful of books—no shopping bags in those days—and return with another armful for the coming week. As the babies slept and later padded around my bench in the park, I did the reading of a lifetime. Mostly on Harry's recommendation I devoured Flaubert and Turgenev, Chekov and more Tolstoi. We both tried to keep up with the new books—Galsworthy's *The Forsyte Saga*, as it came out; Arnold Bennett's Clayhanger trio, Wells, Hardy, Dreiser, even Sherwood Anderson (*Winesburg, Ohio*) and James Branch Cabell (*The Rivet in Grandfather's Neck*). I remember a feeling of dismay, almost of terror, that I would never—*never*—catch up. New books coming out every day, authors one had never heard of, reviewers urging, arguing . . .

Proust was just being translated. *Swann's Way* and *Within a Budding Grove* came out in the early twenties published in small volumes by Thomas Selzer, uncle of our old friends, the Boni boys. Everybody was talking Proust. In 1922 we smuggled in a copy of James Joyce's *Ulysses* from Paris (it was forbidden in the U.S.A.) and gave it as a wedding present to a couple who we knew would prefer it to a silver bowl. And so it was. They reveled in its possession for two years, then rang up to say that they hoped we wouldn't mind if they sold *Ulysses* in order to buy a sun lamp for their little boy who was ill. We had paid the equivalent of $3.50 for the book in Paris, but at its blackmarket price in New York they were able to exchange it for a $45 sun lamp.

I shall never forget the impact upon me of Hemingway's *The Sun Also Rises* in 1927. I read it cold, without any hullabaloo, just because someone had put it in my hand; and I felt as if I'd never read a novel before. It would

be impossible for anyone reading it now for the first time—
after a generation of imitators—to have any comprehension
of the radical freshness that that book had for us then.

This was the stage in publishing when Horace Live-
right was getting out the smart best sellers, and Charles the
First (it's now down to Charles the Third) of Scribners
was bringing over the pick of English books; when Nelson
Doubleday, the somewhat wayward son, was still taking
orders from F. N. ("Effendi" to Joseph Conrad), his father.
Bennett Cerf was working on Wall Street, and Simon &
Schuster hadn't even got together on the first of the crossword puzzle books which put them in business. The book
world was running an even course. But ahead lay adventure.

For us the Big Change came to a head in the middle
twenties. It started up on Lake Mooselookneguntic in
Maine, where the Weisses had given us their lodge for our
honeymoon. There we fished for lake trout and salmon,
bathed in the ice-cold lake, walked through deep forest
paths, and *talked*. Honeymoon couples, I've always noticed,
are distinguishable by their compulsion to talk from the
other very young couples one sees in pleasant places in
springtime. They have so much to tell and to find out—the
kind of people they both like and dislike, their favorite
author, the peculiarities of their families, how they like
their eggs. They don't know a thing about each other's
ordinary tastes, and they're desperate to get acquainted.

So it was with us. Harry had a hundred ideas, and
has continued to have them, cropping up daily and hourly
through the years. But one particular vision, dreamy as he
described it up there in Maine, led quite definitely toward
a path which in a few years became a broad highway.

It had to do with books. The first manifestation to
reach beyond our private conversations was the Little

Leather Library. This was a set of fifteen classics made up
in tiny leather books, about 5″ by 6″. It took some ingenuity
to launch these leather midgets on the market with a capital
of just about four thousand dollars. Harry sold them single-
handed—to Woolworth's, which was then really a "five-
and-ten," and to Whitman's Candy Company where they
inserted one book in each package of candy and called it
"The Library Box." He put them in drugstores on stands—
forerunners of the paperback racks of today.

But the Little Leather Library really arrived when he
sold it by mail.

At this point Harry gave up his job, burned his
bridges behind him and faced the American public. He was
not alone. I've often heard him say that a young man starting out in business needs a partner to bolster him. In this
case it was Max Sackheim, a young Chicago advertising
man who worked at a desk beside Harry at the J. Walter
Thompson Agency. They were both mail-order copywriters,
and now they became partners in the new enterprise. Max
stayed on for a time at the agency. But the Little Leather
Library sales ads emanated from a cell in the Flatiron
Building. There Max's wife Sarah and I addressed envelopes and licked stamps. Evenings the man of the house—
of my house at least—studied bookkeeping, another abso-
lute necessity, as he has always said, for the young man
with a business ahead of him. The bookkeeping method
which he studied was that of the Alexander Hamilton Insti-
tute. He had written the ads for this course of study at the
agency, and sold himself on his own copy.

The list of titles grew to a hundred, and sets were
mailed all over the country in ever increasing numbers. In
time the leather became imitation and a dreadful odor permeated our lives. The printer, the binder, the paper man,
all became our good friends, close old friends who still have

a bond, and sometimes laugh together at those hundreds of seemingly insurmountable problems of long ago.

But the hazy idea which I heard first expressed in a rowboat on Lake Mooselookneguntic was a step beyond mere selling by mail. It concerned book subscription, like magazine subscription: new books to go out through the mail and be delivered with regularity, maybe one book a month, on the customer's doorstep.

The hunger for books which the public displayed in the LLL campaign strengthened this earlier notion. People wanted to read good books, just the way we wanted to ourselves. There weren't good libraries in many towns, people off the beaten track had little access to them, and bookstores obviously weren't doing the job.

It's history now. "Books of the Month" get into the post offices of the tiniest hamlets in the country. Name one, and they'll find you the name of a subscriber: Thistle, Utah; Hope, Arkansas; Slaughter, Kentucky; Bell Buckle, Tennessee; Bunkie, Louisiana . . . But it took organization and change and many a hurdle to arrive. It was always Harry's baby. Max Sackheim dropped out soon to run a successful advertising agency of his own; Robert Haas, the company's first investor and president, left it for publishing (Random House). But Harry stayed on—through the stock market crash, through the Depression, through the war . . .

One of the prime attractions was the roster of judges who chose the books—especially those first judges who were in from the birth. They were personalities as well as good book pickers. They were dearly beloved.

Most people, I think, would put William Allen White among the first ten influential right-thinking men in America in the first third of the twentieth century. He was a

liberal, interviewing picketers at the Lawrence strike in
1908. He was a muckraker, fighting causes in the small but
famous *Emporia Gazette*, published in a town of three
thousand in the very middle of the country, but quoted from
California to New York. He was sent on war missions. He
reported the Peace Conference in Paris in 1919. "Mary
White," the lovely piece he wrote about his sixteen-year-old
daughter who was killed in an accident, is a classic. His
book about Calvin Coolidge, *A Puritan in Babylon*, is a
triumph of objective appraisal.

He was a redhead turning gray, with a round ruddy-
pink face, and blue eyes that really twinkled. Very few
eyes really twinkle, but his did. He came from the "sticks,"
yet he was the complete cosmopolite, always and everywhere at ease.

Bill White's first love was music. He wanted to be a
pianist. And music sustained him spiritually all his life. He
always managed to get to the Philharmonic on his brief New
York visits, and at home he played records. When he was
dying—slowly and painfully—he insisted on getting up
and dressed every evening to listen properly to music. We
sent him the score of *Oklahoma!* just out that year, and the
Schubert C Major String Quintet. It was the Schubert that
he wanted to hear most often, and it was the strains of that
beautiful quintet that he last heard.

But the best thing that ever happened to him, he used
to say, was that he had to give up practicing piano, and
then stop music lessons altogether, when he got a job on a
Kansas City newspaper. "I'd have been a second-rate piano
teacher in a third-rate town."

When he couldn't get to one of the monthly meetings
of the judges he telephoned his comment and his vote.
"Such-and-so," he said of one of the contestants, "is the
dirtiest book I ever read. Not that I was shocked by it. The

fences, barns and outhouse walls of childhood's golden hour gave me great familiarity with the general idea of the book." . . . "Thing-a-ma-bob is just a paper from a woman's club on Flemish art done as a cyclorama. It reads as well forward as backward, and up as well as down." . . . Of another: "As I read it I first thought 'This is symbolism.' But I got to thinking, 'No, this is alcoholism.' My final conclusion is that it is gibberish."

He and his wife Sally came to New York often. Sally was beautiful, with dark eyes and black hair pulled back in smooth severity off her face. Edna Ferber, who was a close friend of the Whites', used her as the physical model for the mother in *So Big*. Later she used "Afternoon of a Faun" as title for one of her most popular stories at Bill White's suggestion. They had just been to the Friday afternoon Philharmonic concert together and heard Toscanini play Debussy's piece of that name.

He emanated good humor. "I have never been bored an hour in my life. I get up every morning wondering what new glamorous thing is going to happen . . ." He had fun. When he went to Moscow he could not get over the excitement in the streets. "Every day it's a football crowd!" In the lobby of the National Hotel, a Russian came up and spoke to him in a pretty good imitation of Midwestern American. The Russian had recognized Bill White and knew the *Emporia Gazette* well enough to quote from an editorial. And why shouldn't he? He had beeen in Leavenworth for years, imprisoned there for extraradical activities.

The Whites were completely taken with the Chinese in 1936, especially the peasants. *They laugh so much! They are so clever! Give them an old radio set, or a victrola and in no time they have it copied down to the last wire!* He returned to Emporia with twenty small white fur muffs to give to "the girls"—office, household, neighbors.

"I prefer brunettes!" he announced one evening emphatically at our dinner table. It was the day of Anita Loos's *Gentlemen Prefer Blondes*. He couldn't have been more tactful. There was his wife with raven hair, his hostess also with black hair, and her daughter the same.

Sally probably read most of the books, then put into his hands the ones she knew he should, or would like to, read. But what an air he gave to that row of judges' heads that topped the Book-of-the-Month Club ads!

Heywood Broun was another who didn't read the books unless Ruth Hale, his forthright wife, saw to it that he did. But he came to all the meetings. They never expected him but he was always there.

The famous description of Broun "looking like an unmade bed" was slightly belied at those meetings. True, his necktie was a string knotted about an inch below the collar button, and once he came wearing shoes that weren't mates. But the shoelaces, which usually hung loose, were tied for the judges' meetings. His unruly hair was plastered down. And though he was notoriously late for all appointments, he got to the BOMC on time.

The explanation seems to be that when Broun was a boy in Horace Mann High School, at 120th and Broadway, he was sometimes sent to the office of Mr. Prettyman, the principal, possibly for purposes of discipline. At any rate, while awaiting Mr. Prettyman's pleasure, he would find himself sitting opposite the principal's secretary, a charming lady with bright eyes and curly hair, by name of Miss Dorothy Canfield. Now he was New York's headline reporter, but facing Dorothy Canfield at the Book-of-the-Month judges' table he was still the uneasy boy hoping to cut a figure of which she would approve.

Sometimes we played bridge with Heywood and Ruth. We all liked to play. Heywood would have squirmed in misery if he'd been faced with an evening of talk. But with just four of us, dinner, and a couple of hours of bridge, he was fulfilling a duty which was endurable and sometimes mildly pleasurable. He'd rather have been in an aisle seat at a show, out of which he could walk at the exact minute he wanted to—that's for sure. Or playing poker with the Thanatopsis Club, which wouldn't be meeting a weekday night anyway. Or drinking. Or gazing at a pretty girl. Way back in the Washington Square Players days I remember how he loved to look at Lydia Lopokova, the Russian ballerina who later married, not Heywood as beyond a doubt he hoped she would but Lord Keynes, brilliant English economist, at that time not yet a viscount. She was tiny enough to sit in Heywood's big hand.

As for drinking. He used to bring along a small medicine bottle of gin—that small, I suppose, because he was satisfied that our evening would not be a long one. You wouldn't think he'd bother to hide it, and go into another room to take a swig. He fooled no one, and by that time there was plenty of liquor on hand in everyone's house. But he had a respectable bourgeois bringing-up and it kept getting in his way.

One time playing a defense hand in bridge, he made a costly mistake. It concerned a queen of spades. Probably he didn't cover his opponent's jack with his queen, his partner could not make good her ten-spot, and the other side made an undeserved game. He couldn't get it off his mind. If only he'd played that queen! Three hands later he was still muttering. Finally Ruth Hale shouted at him, "Forget the goddamned queen of spades and play your hand!"

They were devoted in their way. Ruth knew every little weakness of big lumbering Heywood. She probably knew every little girl that sat in his lap and every little drink that passed his lips. But she didn't protest or interfere. Sometimes she did lean over the table to tidy his hair, reaching into his coat pocket to get a comb.

When she died, though they had long been separated, he wrote a lovely piece about her in the *World-Telegram*.

My best friend died yesterday . . . She was not my severest critic. Her tolerance was broad to the mass of mediocre stuff the newspaper hack is bound to produce in seventeen years. Nobody else, I suppose, ever gave me such warm support and approbation for those afternoons when I did my best. She made me feel ashamed when I faltered, and I suppose in seventeen years practically every word I wrote was set down with the feeling that Ruth Hale was looking over my shoulder.

It would be a desperately lonely world if I did not feel personality is of such tough fiber that in some manner it must survive and does survive. I still feel that she is looking over my shoulder.

I think that the greatest joy Harry got out of all his relationships in the book world, then and now and all the years between, was his friendship with Dorothy Canfield.

She was a very pretty woman with wayward hair, sky-blue eyes, a piquant nose. She was small and moved swiftly. She had a man's mind but a woman's charm. She had profound understanding, delving deep below the surface in her own character, in the characters she created, no doubt in her friends. But she was light as a breeze. Her wit was sharp and her laugh rippled.

She was a sensational linguist. Completely bilingual in French and English, she also translated Papini's *Life of Christ* from the Italian, and all the Montessori educational works which revolutionized the approach to child study in this country. She was fluent in German, and spoke Norwegian and Danish—how well I don't know. She was a famous figure in Norway, and was also responsible for intro-

ducing the works of her friend Isak Dinesen, the Baroness
Blixen, to the American public.

Like Bill White, Dorothy Canfield too had wanted to
be a musician. She studied the violin and planned to make
it her career. But a defect in hearing showed up when she
was in her teens which deflected her from music platform
to library. Her father had been a librarian, a teacher and a
college president. Her mother was a painter. And Dorothy
as a young girl found herself at loose ends in Paris where
the artist mother quite forgot her daughter in the world of
paints and brushes. Dorothy went to school over there and
after school sat in corners of studios alone, waiting. When
she finally got into the class of Professor Meyer, famous
philologist at the Sorbonne, she found that all the drabness
of her Parisian life had not been in vain. Here was her career! Hers would be a scholar's life.

Undoubtedly it would have been, had she not just at
this point met John Fisher, handsome American fullback
from the Columbia team of 1905, and married him. So
Dorothy had a family, and she became a writer—one of the
most widely read American authors of her day, both in her
own country and throughout Europe. Her books were particularly popular in Russia and built up a nice pile of rubles
which she never got there to collect; and a whole generation
of Americans were brought up on *Understood Betsy*, *The
Bent Twig*, *The Brimming Cup*.

By the time we knew her she had settled in Arlington,
Vermont, home of the Canfields, glad to be back after many
years in France on the ancestral soil, with her progeny at
her knee. In spite of her cosmopolitanism, Dorothy Canfield
was as much a part of Vermont as the ferns on the mountainside and the blueberries in the pasture. *The Vermont
Tradition*, a biography you might say of the state, is one of
her last works and, I think, her very finest book.

It was a lively household that she ran. All four—John,

Dorothy, son Jim and daughter Sally—skied, played tennis, walked through the beautiful birch forest on the next mountain north, climbed Red Mountain, and roamed the pine woods which she and John had planted. We ourselves saw these pines grow from saplings to heavy timber trees.

Dorothy and her son were great companions. They used to drive about in Jim's coupe, top down. Early mornings when it is so good to be up with the sun in Vermont, they read Greek together. Jim's death during the war—in the Philippines, where he was an Army doctor—was the first shadow to fall on the Fishers. A dark shadow, from which it took all their power to emerge.

Dorothy moved in a glow of love. She never lost the feminine charm that made Heywood Broun tie up his shoelaces, and brought her old beaux back to her side year after year. We knew three of these swains, elderly in our day, three of her contemporaries who spent every summer near her. One lived nearby and never married, another lived in New York and came up every summer. He, too, did not marry. And comfortably, beloved, by her side was of course John. The four of them all fast friends.

In still later years, thirty years after she was first a BOMC judge, the foursome of contemporaries was only slightly changed. One of the old beaux died. That left Dorothy and John, the New Yorker (still spending his summers in Vermont) and Jim Canfield, Dorothy's older brother and her vivid counterpart. Nearly every evening during the summer these four sat in the Fisher living room, with its French chairs and good pictures, reading aloud. They read books that one or the other of them had missed in the course of a long reading life, or that they had grown rusty on, or had forgotten. I'd love a list of those books. Once when we were there we found them reading Trevelyan, another time Montaigne, Muller's *The Loom of History*. The man from New York was a frustrated actor who read beautifully and they all contributed wit and comment. It was a rare idyl in the so seldom light-hearted downstream of life.

Dorothy died in 1958, and John carried on through a cold Vermont winter, alone except for Marguerite, the French Canadian housekeeper who had been with them so many, many years. He stayed on because of Marguerite, whom he felt he couldn't abandon. But he was lonely. In November of that year Jim Canfield died. His eighty-fifth birthday was November 10. His father and grandfather had both lived to be eighty-five. "I've almost made it!" he said on the ninth when he knew he was slipping fast, but he died before midnight.

John went to Jim's funeral. He was pale. He looked ghastly. Three days later he died. There wasn't any incentive left. Sally, their daughter, was completely caught up in her life and large family many miles away. Son Jim was gone. Dolly. And now Jim.

Dorothy's mind and Harry's met in many places. In *The Deepening Stream*, the novel she had just finished when we first knew her, the heroine had a religious experience which struck an answering chord in his nature. Though he has never been a churchgoer, Harry is deeply concerned with religion. The book which he reads over and over again is not the Bible, but a well-thumbed volume of William James's *Varieties of Religious Experience*. In the heroine of *The Deepening Stream* he recognized Dorothy herself. As he said, only one who had gone through such a spiritual revelation could possibly have written with that awareness. It added a depth of understanding that grew and intensified with their long friendship.

The other two judges of the Book-of-the-Month in those early days were Henry Canby and Christopher Morley. Henry was a stabilizer. A good critic, not only of books but of life; a true naturalist whose book on Thoreau is maybe the best of the many; the perfect traveler, with curiosities and an open mind. Many of the most charming spots we came to know in later years, in the Caribbean, in Ireland, in Austria, were first described to us by Henry and Marian Canby. He was also one of the most actively humane men I have ever known. When the refugees from Hitler began to come into this country by the thousands, the Canby home became a center for mid-European intellectuals deprived of their homes and their universities. There was nothing official about this, none of the drab compulsion of social work. The Canby's social evenings consisted of good companionship and stimulating conversation in German and/or English, sandwiches, perhaps a wine cup, and laughter. The Europeans met Americans who were interested in the same things that interested them. Their self-esteem got a boost. Scattered about the country in colleges and professional offices are many grateful people right now who will tell you that it was through the Canby connections that they got work, or were encouraged to continue study, or were helped to go on with their art.

Chris Morley stands out in my memory, not for the accomplishments and books you'll find in the biographies of him but, first, for his esoteric vocabulary, which flabbergasted me—I always leaned on a dictionary when reading him; second, for his novel *Kitty Foyle*, probably the last work he would wish to be remembered by; and last, for the little oasis outside the honky-tonk of New York which he promoted at Hoboken.

The year was 1927, and feeling against Prohibition was running high. Crime was on the increase, flappers were rampant, and the taste for gin had in no way diminished with the years. The highbrow attitude was to ridicule, to thumb the nose at legality and treat it as impudently as the traffic would bear. Mencken was a leader in the demolition squad. And Chris and the three-hours-for-lunch club backed him up.

It was this latter group with Chris Morley as steersman that resurrected the old Rialto theater in Hoboken and put on two naughty shows out of the mid-nineteenth century, *After Dark: Neither Maid Nor Wife Nor Widow* and *The Black Crook.* Hoboken saloons and restaurants were wide open, and New Yorkers crowded into the dockhands' back rooms to eat and drink. The street in front of the theater was roped off, and every night was a first night— for celebrities, clothes, bright lights, general hilarity. For a time Hoboken became the smartest spot in the metropolitan area.

Christopher Morley was a scholar and a poet, and a writer of fanciful, sometimes beautiful prose: *Where the Blue Begins, Thunder on the Left, I Know a Secret.* But *Kitty Foyle* was down to earth—a straight old-fashioned novel about a white-collar Philadelphia girl from the wrong side of the tracks, and her affair with her boss. Unmarred by big words or too brilliant sallies, it is a realistic love story hovering somewhere between Kathleen Norris and Theodore Dreiser. I read it through a long rainy day, enthralled.

All the judges had extensive correspondence with Mollie Stoller, their special secretary at the BOMC. At the end of one of his long letters, in which he praised her efficiency and her wealth of information, Chris asked Miss Stoller to turn the letter over to Mr. Scherman. "I never hesitate to take liberties with him," wrote Chris, "because he and I were both married the same day, June 3, 1914. *That's* something you didn't know!"

John Marquand overlapped the first group of judges. He was far and away the best-looking judge the BOMC ever had. And the best dressed in his carefully careless tweeds. He was Boston. He was his own topnotch character. They tell me that the judges couldn't wait to hear what Marquand had to say about each month's crop of books— and the *way* he'd say it. Frequently he was in a choleric rage, a bit of it genuine, much of it play-acting, all of it part and parcel of the novelist *par excellence* that he was—the satirist who reproduced and commented on the American social scene with such sagacity and devastating wit. He was an enormously popular writer. His novels sold like wildfire. But his passing is too close to us right now for the critics to gauge his place in the ranks of the immortals. It is always that way. For a time they forget. But there is already a stirring, and the prediction is that in the long view Marquand's novels will be close to the top of the ladder of true Americana.

He died in his sleep the night of July 16, 1960. On July 14 he was at a meeting of the judges, gay and vociferous as usual, and on July 18 I received a letter he had written the day he died. He was pleased that I liked *Timothy Dexter Revisited*. That was his last book, not fiction, but he was already well started on a new novel, he said, and very excited. Too, too bad that we shall never see it!

On Harry's desk are three pictures, one of Dorothy Canfield, one of his mother, which I sanctimoniously put there, and the third of Wesley Mitchell, famous economist. Of all his books the one he treasures most, next to *Varieties of Religious Experience*, is Wesley Mitchell's *Business Cycles*. These two books are the counterpoint that makes up the intricate harmony of his intellectual life.

One day walking down Park Avenue he met Dr. Mitchell. They greeted each other enthusiastically. "Where are you going so fast?" asked Harry. "Home," said Dr.

Mitchell. "I'm an old man in a hurry!" He was hurrying to
get the next book done—his last.

Probably of all his reading the Mitchell book has had
the greatest influence on Harry's thinking. It underlies the
study which has engrossed him all the years I have known
him, and which he never neglected for business, however
pressing. How did he take his pleasure on weekends and
free evenings the first twenty years of our married life?
Reading economic and financial journals and pamphlets,
taking notes on long yellow-pad sheets, pondering in long
silence. How did he spend the month of April, 1937, in
breath-takingly beautiful Dubrovnik? Revising the final
draft of a long book of his own which was the harvest of
these studies.

*The Promises Men Live By: A New Approach to Eco-
nomics* was published in February, 1938. Publication was
set for a Tuesday in the last week of the month, and the
publishers had sent out advance copies to a select number of
people who would be likely to appreciate its significance. It
was a serious, important book.

In the meantime our household was wordless.

The Sunday before the book was to come out was cold.
A fine mist was blowing across the Hudson and beating
against our windows. Late in the afternoon Harry went for
a walk down Riverside Drive to clear his head and probably
to shake off the pall of worry. He was no doubt facing the
fear that so many authors say they feel at this point: suppose the reviews are all bad . . . suppose there are no reviews . . . suppose no one reads the book at all! The
waste of it all! The terrible, terrible letdown! Of course I
didn't know for sure. As I said, a deadly quiet prevailed in
our home.

I was alone in the apartment, unable to help in any
way, grim and blue. When the telephone rang there was

only I to answer. "Is this the home of Harry Scherman?" "Yes." "The Harry Scherman who wrote a book called *The Promises Men Live By?*" "*Yes!*" "May I speak with Mr. Scherman?" "He is out, but I am his wife. May I give him a message?" "This is Bernard Baruch speaking. I do not know your husband, but when I got home yesterday I found a book on my hall table. I get lots of books. But I did pick this one up—maybe the title. And I started reading. I read it through all last evening and today. I have just finished it and I want to say that I think this is the final word on the economy of debt. I congratulate your husband. He has done a magnificent job!"

That is the kind of conversation of which a wife remembers every word and every inflection. I can't recall a moment that has ever given me the wild joy of that short telephone talk. It was the peak of my married life.

Later that year, quite out of space, came word from a different world. Hu Shih, the Chinese ambassador to the U.S.A., professor at Peking University, philosopher and poet, wrote Harry a letter in which he said that for the first time in a long life he understood the theory of economics. *The Promises* did it.

These are only isolated expressions out of high praise from all quarters. But they were special triumphs. Just lately (1962) an AP reporter interviewed a man who lives on Wall Street (at this writing he is just moving out!)— the only man in many years who maintained a dwelling on Wall Street. He had a four-story house with a large library, of which he considers *The Promises Men Live By* the most important book. Every time he passes a second-hand bookstore, he told the young reporter, he goes in to see if they have a copy. Every copy that he can get his hands on he sends out to someone who he thinks should read it.

The Promises was followed by some shorter books

and many articles in the same field, and fields not far re-
moved. The titles are all come-ons: *One-Legged Nation
. . . The Real Danger in Our Gold . . . Inflation in One
Easy Lesson . . . What Is This War About? . . . The
Last Best Hope of Earth . . .*

XIII

HOME

In New York things have changed. The Hudson River no longer flows majestically below our window. Now we live in the center of the busiest city in the world, surrounded by eight million people, towering masses of glass and concrete, crime, noise, traffic jams, air pollution—and we would not live anywhere else. Coming back each Sunday night from the green haven of New Jersey, we sigh contentedly as we drive across the asphalt of Fifty-seventh Street.

This has been my own sentiment for a long, long time, but of my companion's I've not been entirely sure. For years I have avoided inducing a definite decision on a subject that sooner or later must be faced: should we sometime "retire"? Should we end our days in serenity in the country beside the pond with wild geese, under stately spruces, amid the fragrance of honeysuckle and the twinkle of fireflies? Or should we see it through right here? I wanted to know, but I didn't want to face a showdown. Then, one Sunday evening, driving along that same street, Harry said, quite out of the blue, "This is home, isn't it?" It came like a reprieve.

When we moved from the homey reaches of Riverside Drive to our present apartment, I felt as if I were living in sin. The wide view out the back windows was fairyland, towers rose in beautiful irregularity—the Chrysler, the Empire State, the Metropolitan, no two alike, uneven in their heights, an entrancing glorified San Gemingano. We could even see the downtown towers on clear days (and the days were clearer then!) and the three downtown bridges to Brooklyn. The pattern of lights at night was breath-taking, or better yet on late winter afternoons when office buildings were still open and lights shone from a thousand windows against the raspberry red of a January sunset. With maybe a new moon, or the evening star.

We breakfasted in a room with two walls of glass looking out on the East River, the sun pouring in on us with glorious frequency: if you doubt that New York is a sunny city, ask any visitor from London or Paris or Zurich or San Francisco. There we have sat for twenty-five years in a fragrant morning mélange of coffee, bacon, toast, *The New York Times* and the *Herald-Tribune.* For eighteen of these years a third chair was occupied—by Suki, a Siamese cat. Suki shared our lives as few outsiders could believe. He went with us to and from the country every weekend, he conversed with us in a loud Asiatic voice, he understood us perfectly and we understood him.

On a balcony overlooking the living room of the apartment is the dining room, scene of somewhat more sedate little dinners than those that Susie and the Browns used to serve us in the old days. There is less table-thumping than

In the argumentative thirties, more of a variety of guests. You can't live on and on in a city of eight million without accumulating an ever-growing number of acquaintances, many of whom become friends, a few of whom become close companions. With us it has been people in the publishing world, musical characters, a handful of the old Bohemians, and close friends out of our premarital life, Harry's from Philadelphia, mine from New England. My college roommate Nina Weiss who introduced me to New York, is still my close friend, and her daughter is the close friend of my daughter. There is a bond between us that neither of us takes for granted. We are both actively grateful for each other. I know I am. When I answer the telephone and hear her voice, what a lift I get! and how much the same, I imagine, does she respond to mine.—As our children have grown up, the generations have mingled so thoroughly that I sometimes forget to which one we belong ourselves, which is stimulating, and at the same time very comforting.

Our choice of an evening is six around the table, preferably people who like to talk and to hear what others have to say; who sit over coffee for hours, talking shop, gossiping, philosophizing maybe, and leave unwillingly at midnight.

Sometimes we have a musical evening. When Tom lived at home there'd be members of his orchestra playing trios for fun, quartets, sextettes, all the way up to nonettes, with Tom at the piano. But those evenings have long since been transferred to his home; and what we now have—if any—is a musical free-for-all. Someone sits down at the piano who plays by ear and can give you anything you ask for, and everybody sings—songs of the twenties and the thirties, and way back earlier. Everyone, including grandchildren, seems to know them. In its small way it's a very satisfactory continuity.

The section in which we live is smarter than what we knew for so many years on upper Broadway, but it's still *gemütlich*. I seldom go out without running into a friend. Bloomingdale's is our big drygoods store (as a neighbor once said, she'd like to be laid out in Bloomingdale's because all her friends would see her). The new school at Fifty-seventh and Second Avenue is "our" school. I know eleven or twelve stores in this village intimately and am known in them myself, in spite of an undeniable fascination for the new supermarket which is insinuating itself into the heart of every woman in the neighborhood. The small stores are on their way out. "I'm the last of the Mohegans," said the Jewish watchmaker in a strong Yiddish accent. He has just moved away from our corner because the old building where he was located is being torn down and he can't afford the new rents. The Swedish delicatessen has gone the same way. The Italian fruit man occupies a decrepit corner store on Second Avenue in a dilapidated old building, the owner no doubt holding out for a top price in this suddenly flourishing neighborhood. In the meantime the door handle is gone. A red chalk arrow indicates where you push to get out, and I find that I relish it just because it is inefficient, unchromium-plated, old. The shoemaker is a Greek and he commutes to the city from Babylon, getting up at five-thirty every morning, year in and year out, reaching home about nine at night. All around his shop bulldozers are pounding down the buildings, at either side of him and behind; Con Edison is tearing up the street in front to make new outlets for new gadgets. But he is holding on to his lease. Indoors he polishes your shoes with imperturbability, and whirls the dust off your husband's fedora. Some of Second Avenue's early simplicity still lies there untouched. It's like a handful of long-stemmed violets, without tin foil.

When we first moved in, the El was still running, its

roar was like the beating of waves on the shore, and we minded it no more than if nature produced it. All the familiar city sounds grow pleasant to our urban ears. Waking up in the night I can tell within a half-hour what time it is from the sound or lack of sound. The quietest half-hour is between 3:15 and 3:45, and it is much less quiet at 6:30 than it is at 5:30. Tires on wet pavement make a sizzling splash, and the noiselessness when snow has fallen wakes one up. On a downright rainy morning the doormen's whistles are a symphony of mingled notes—sharp and impatient, long and penetrating.

Walking in New York is entertainment of a high order, and as Boswell said of walking in London, "I think with a kind of wonder that I see it for nothing." Like Boswell I don't walk for exercise so much as for pleasure and curiosity. I've never tried walking the entire length of Broadway—it's thirteen and a half miles—but it might be a good walk. My preference is for the odd corners—the East River docks at lunchtime with the sun shining straight down and the high downtown buildings protecting you from the wind. The big fishing boats are empty then, swinging slightly with the current. Or better still, the fish market itself at seven in the morning, with breakfast across the street at Sweet's (Lake and Anderson's) along with a ship's captain or two.

Battery Park would be a revelation to a lot of New Yorkers if they saw fit to pay it a visit. Its greenery is fresher by far than that of any other park because of the sea, its view of the harbor is at eye level, and the incoming ships seem near enough to touch. Hundreds of tugs chug around, and nowadays commuters with cash can taxi by speedboat from Westchester, Connecticut and Long Island. —Coney Island is not what you'd call an odd corner, but it's a fine place to walk, five miles of boardwalk with a terrace restaurant at the Aquarium from which you can watch Olaf the walrus while you're eating.

Year after year I have walked over Brooklyn Bridge. I've taken elderly New England visitors and small grand-children. The view toward New York at sunset is a lovely pattern—the slanting diagonal of the skyscrapers seen through the close vertical cables of the bridge itself; the gray stone of the buildings, the ephemeral color of sky and cloud, and the metallic shine of the water. Al Smith was born and brought up in the shadow of Brooklyn Bridge. The big solid anchorage towers were built the year he was born, 1873, and the bridge was opened in 1883 when he was just under ten. "The bridge and I grew up together," he used to say. On the first Saturday after its opening the whole Smith family journeyed across, each paying the walk-er's toll, which was one cent. Now there's a big housing project near the bridge. It covers old Cherry Street where George Washington lived in America's first White House, where before that there was a cherry orchard; where our Catalan friend and restaurateur El Padrone held forth dur-ing Spanish Civil War days, and where, until it was re-habilitated, there was a deep dark slum. It's now called the Alfred E. Smith House, and though he would have been nostalgic he would have approved.

I wander around like a tourist—even to churches. Our churches are not Gothic cathedrals, but some of them are uniquely New York. The Paulist Fathers' Church on Fifty-ninth Street and Ninth Avenue has a Standford White altar. The Church of the Ascension on lower Fifth Avenue has St. Gaudens' angels and John La Farge's finest mural. St. Stephen's on East Twenty-eighth Street has fourteen splendid columns that once were masts in nineteenth-cen-tury sailing vessels. On the steeple of the Dutch Reformed

Church at Twenty-ninth and Fifth Avenue is a rooster brought over from Holland to Nieuw Amsterdam.

The big day at Trinity Church, at the head of Wall Street, is Ascension Thursday, with a resplendent procession and very fine music. The best church music in the city, however, I'd say, is at St. Mary the Virgin's, in the theatrical quarter. It's High Church Episcopal, so high that a Catholic cousin of mine who came to New York frequently on business, went there every Sunday to Mass until someone questioned the procedure. "Where do we pay our fifteen cents?" I always go there on Good Friday to hear the Tenebrae sung. It is a long service made up of responses between priest and choir. For two hours one is lulled by the monotonous chanting. On the altar are many lighted candles, and after each chapter of the Litany, a single candle is snuffed out. Gradually the church dims. As the candles go out, so do the lights in the ceiling and on the pillars. Maybe it is the proximity of the theater world that makes the Tenebrae so particularly dramatic at St. Mary's. One by one the candles go out, till only a single candle is left lighted on the altar, only a single light in the church. Then the chanting stops. With a crash of cymbals behind the altar you know that the end has come. Christ has died, and the church is in total darkness. The large congregation files out silently, the church still completely dark.

One half of our married life has been spent in this present apartment. The first half, made up of an infinite number of remembered faces and happenings is a mosaic in which each piece fits almost perfectly into place. The second half has glided along so smoothly as to leave no perceptible mark. It seems hardly more than an incident. A full generation has grown up around us that doesn't know how New

York looked in 1938 when we made the big move—in fact, we have to hunt a bit to find it ourselves.

We still have breakfast on the porch. But the view of the East River is now obscured by a twenty-story apartment building. And there is no Suki. He died just short of his nineteenth birthday, unobtrusively, in a dark closet. The boy on the back elevator on which Suki used to ride up and down frequently *pour le sport*, asked if he could come in to see him once more. The superintendent came up to pay his respects. The tenants knew Suki and spoke of him with affection. It was like a wake.

The view out the south window has changed too. The beautiful towers are gone—not really gone but covered and blurred among solid high faceless buildings, each indistinguishable from the next.

But there is nothing to be gained by crying for the past. New York hasn't grown old. It has grown new. Some of the old enchantment has vanished just in the past four or five years. *Our* enchantment. But as someone said of the ultra-modern music: the folks who will like it haven't yet been born.

BERNARDINE KIELTY was born and brought up in northeastern Massachusetts, went to Wellesley, and would undoubtedly have been a dyed-in-the-wool New Englander had she not chanced to get a job in New York immediately after college. There she has lived ever since. She is married to Harry Scherman, author and publisher, and has a son and a daughter, both with careers: one a musician, the other a writer. She was on the staff of *Story* magazine; later edited a large anthology, *A Treasury of Short Stories;* had a book column on the *Ladies' Home Journal* for seventeen years—a cherished experience; wrote four books for young readers—one on art, the others, historical biographies; and has through it all been a reader for the Book-of-the-Month Club.